I0437164

THE CHARM OF LATIN AMERICA

ECONOMIC AND CULTURAL IMPRESSIONS

VITO TANZI

IUNIVERSE, INC.
NEW YORK   BLOOMINGTON

The Charm of Latin America
Economic and Cultural Impressions

Copyright © 2010 by Vito Tanzi

All rights reserved. No part of this book may be used or reproduced by any means, graphic, electronic, or mechanical, including photocopying, recording, taping or by any information storage retrieval system without the written permission of the publisher except in the case of brief quotations embodied in critical articles and reviews.

The views expressed in this work are solely those of the author and do not necessarily reflect the views of the publisher, and the publisher hereby disclaims any responsibility for them.

iUniverse books may be ordered through booksellers or by contacting:

iUniverse
1663 Liberty Drive
Bloomington, IN 47403
www.iuniverse.com
1-800-Authors (1-800-288-4677)

Because of the dynamic nature of the Internet, any Web addresses or links contained in this book may have changed since publication and may no longer be valid.

ISBN: 978-1-4401-8384-3 (sc)
ISBN: 978-1-4401-8386-7 (dj)
ISBN: 978-1-4401-8385-0 (ebk)

Printed in the United States of America

iUniverse rev. date: 12/14/2009

For my wife, Maria,
who shared many of these experiences with me
and made them much more pleasant

The World Is A Book And
Those Who Do Not Travel
Read Only One Page
--Saint Augustine

In This World Which Runs and Is Silent,
I Want More Communications,
Other Languages, Other Signs,
I Want To Know This World

--Pablo Neruda

CONTENTS

PREFACE

My contacts with the Latin American region go back five decades. They started almost by accident. I am not from Latin America, but rather was born in Italy. I have spent much of my adult life in Washington, D.C. In 1962, when I was a graduate student in economics at Harvard, I got a summer job with the Organization of American States (OAS), the political organization located in Washington that comprises the countries of the Americas. At that time it had received a large amount of money from the Kennedy Administration to promote economic development in Latin America. The program of assistance was called *Alliance for Progress* and required the hiring of many economists from the member countries. That summer I went to Washington to work as an assistant to a gentleman from El Salvador, Alvaro Magaña, who later became president of that country. He was then head of an office called Joint Tax Program. The office was charged with promoting tax reform in Latin America. It was my first introduction to Latin America.

Three years later, having completed my PhD, I returned to Washington to teach, first at the George Washington University, and later at the American University. During that period I became a consultant to the same OAS office where I had worked in the Summer of 1962. I kept both positions until 1974, when I went to work for the International Monetary Fund (IMF). During those years I had my first opportunities to visit several Latin American countries. I acquired some knowledge about Latin America and developed a long run interest in the region. In those years I met many interesting people from Latin America, some of whom would go back to their countries and occupy important positions. I also learned enough Spanish to be able to read, understand, and even lecture in that language.

In 1974, I accepted an attractive offer to work for the IMF. I resigned from my tenured professorship and quit my consulting position with the OAS. I would spend the next 27 years with the IMF. A few years after joining the IMF, I was promoted Director of the Fund's Fiscal Affairs Department, a large department responsible for following fiscal developments among the Fund's member countries. The Fund's member countries kept increasing in number. By the time I left the Fund, 184 countries had become members. They included all the countries of Latin America and the Caribbean, with the exception of Cuba.

My work in this new position was no longer focused exclusively on Latin America but extended to the whole membership. My job required me to visit various countries frequently. However, because of my continuing interest in Latin America, I followed developments there more closely than in other regions and visited Latin American countries more frequently than those of other regions.

During these years, I developed a growing appreciation for the history, the culture, the people, and the physical beauty of the region. I read many books on Latin America and tried to visit museums, churches, and other interesting sites whenever I had a chance. During these years I also developed interests in photography and in naïf art. I met several Latin American painters, and my collection of paintings grew considerably over the years. I also started collecting old keys. My photos improved with time and some even won prizes at photographic exhibitions. I was also thrilled when one was bought by the World Bank and placed on the cover of a published report on the environment.

The visits to the countries were linked to various professional activities: to discuss programs of financial assistance that the countries were negotiating with the IMF, to provide technical advice to the countries' governments on fiscal reforms that they were planning to make, to participate in conferences, or simply to give invited lectures. During this period, the University of Cordoba in Argentina gave me an honorary degree. I spent many hours in planes, airports, and hotels and became a truly global economist and a kind of jet-age Marco Polo. My great curiosity to see new places, including uncomfortable ones, continually made this work fascinating even when it was tiring and occasionally dangerous. I always tried to add some extra vacation days to my technical missions to learn about the countries.

Many of the memories of these trips have by now been absorbed by the black hole of time. For others, vague impressions remain of places, people, and events, even though the details have vanished. In some cases, however, the places, the people, or the events had made strong enough impressions on me that, even after many years, I am still able to dig them out from the deepest recesses of my brain. I discovered that, with a determined effort at recollection, and at what could be called a process of mental archeology, some memories could be dug out, polished and presented in ways that could interest and entertain others. I came to believe that the material that I had accumulated over the many years, linked as it was to the places I had visited (and at the times I had been there) and helped by the privileged professional positions that had given me access to many important people, was unique and could not be duplicated by others. I, thus, began to consider the possibility that one day I would use that material to write a book not for specialists but for general readers.

The opportunity came in recent years when, after spending a couple of years in Rome as a member of the Italian government, and a few more years in Washington as a consultant to the Inter-American Development Bank, I found myself, for the first time in decades, with some free time. I started writing a book that would cover my experiences worldwide. However, I soon realized that such a book would be too long and too diverse. The alternative was to write more than one book.

I started with a book on Argentina, the country I had visited more often, and about which I had more memories, extending over 40 years. During these years, Argentina had gone through various dramatic events. I wrote a short book that was published in English, Spanish and Italian with three different titles: *Argentina: an Economic Chronicle*, *Historia Fiscal de la Argentina: de Perón al FMI*, and *Questione di Tasse: La Lezione dall'Argentina*. The readers of this book found it interesting and pleasant to read. It attracted good reviews and encouraged me to continue with this kind of writing.

The second book dealt with a different part of the world, Asia. It was published in 2008 with the title: *Peoples, Places, and Policies: China,*

Japan, and Southeast Asia. Half of this book was about China. That part provided an impressionistic and highly readable account of the phenomenal economic development of that country since 1985, the first year I had visited it. At that time it was still a very poor and much disorganized country. It would change dramatically in the following years. I have visited it annually since then and saw the incredible changes going on. It is like seeing a fast-paced action movie. That book also described my visits to Japan, Korea, Hong Kong, and Indonesia and highlighted some interesting cultural traits. It was again a book written for the general public and not a technical book. Hopefully, it was fun and informative to read. It combined economic and cultural impressions and related several interesting stories.

The present book, *The Charm of Latin America: Economic and Cultural Impressions*, is similar in style to the other two books. It deals with five countries: Brazil, Peru, Chile, Costa Rica, and Guatemala. The one unifying theme in the book is the Latin American region. The treatment of Brazil, Peru, and Chile is extensive. It describes how I saw these countries change over some four decades. The coverage of Costa Rica and Guatemala is limited to one chapter each. The book tries to convey a holistic view of the region. It describes economic developments and cultural aspects, visits to famous tourist sites, such as Machu Picchu, Patagonia, Ouro Preto, and the desert of Atacama, providing some minimum historical information. It attempts to capture the essence, the beauty, and the peculiarity of the region in a way that books or travel guides generally fail to do. It should be added that much of the book is the outcome of direct impressions and experiences and not of hours spent in libraries. It has, thus, a freshness that is normally missing in more technical books.

The Charm of Latin America is written for general readers with some interest in Latin America's economic and cultural aspects. It is not written for people who want to learn about specific aspects of it. Because of my professional background in economics, the book contains many economic observations. However, they are always in a style, and related to aspects, that general readers would be able to understand. It should also appeal to those who travel to the regions because of its descriptions of some beautiful places, not all well known. For example, as an Italian, I was very impressed by the beauty of some seventeenth and eighteenth century churches. I thought that they were as beautiful as some of the churches that one finds in Rome. I very much hope that the readers will enjoy reading this book and will come to appreciate this incredibly beautiful and diverse area of the world.

In conclusion, I would like to express my deep appreciation to Luiz Villela and Bernardo Weaver for reading parts of the book, for providing some information, and for correcting some errors, to Marcilio Marquez Moreira for introducing me to the fascinating story of the Casa dos Contos in Ouro Preto, to Eugenio Ferraz for giving me his beautiful book on the Casa, and to Paulo Páiva for facilitating a splendid visit to Belo Horizonte and especially to Ouro Preto. I would also like to express my deep gratitude to Francesca Caparas for her help with the editing of the book and to Jesusa Hilario for patiently typing many drafts of the manuscript.

Vito Tanzi
Bethesda, Maryland
September 2009

PART 1

BRAZIL

CHAPTER 1

BRAZIL: IN THE 1960S AND 1970S

Over the last four decades, I have visited Brazil many times on behalf of international organizations or on personal trips to attend conferences. The earliest trips, in the period between 1965 and 1973, were on behalf of the Organization of American States (OAS). Thanks to money made available through the Kennedy-Johnson program called *Alliance for Progress,* the OAS created a large department of economics that prepared economic reports on the Latin American countries. For several years these reports competed with those prepared by the World Bank and the International Monetary Fund (IMF). They played a role in allocating U.S. financial assistance to Latin American countries. For a few years that department was very active, attracted competent people to work for it, and did good work. Some of the people who had worked there became presidents of Panama and El Salvador, and others became ministers in some Latin American countries.

In the early 1970s, under a different administration, the United States lost interest in the OAS, funding for its activities was reduced, and the best people left. Furthermore, the institution went back to its more traditional political role, not having been able to find other missions that could attract the interest and the financing of the American government. In some ways, the U.S. government has often been like the sun for international institutions and especially for those located in Washington. While the sun shines, the institutions prosper; when the sun stops shining, the institutions do not die, they just go in hibernation.

On numerous occasions between 1965 and 1973, I traveled to Rio de Janeiro, where most government offices were still located before they moved to the new capital, Brasília. Rio was then a paradise for visitors, located in one of the truly great natural settings in the world and rivaling other similarly situated cities such as San Francisco, Sydney, Naples, Cape Town, and Hong Kong. Its natural beauty was complemented by the charm of its population and especially of the female side. As some would say at the time, Portugal's greatest gift to the world was the mulattas, or *cariocas* (Rio female natives of mixed racial background). The captain of the first Portuguese expedition to visit Rio in 1503, Gonçalves Coelho, built a Stone House before returning to Europe. The local people started calling that house *carioca*, or "White man's house," in their language. Today the female citizens of Rio are called *cariocas* after that small stone house, and they crowd the beautiful beaches that make Rio famous, mainly Copacabana, Ipanema and Botafogo. At the time of my visits, Astrud Gilberto's rendition of "The girl from Ipanema" was a famous international hit song that could be heard all over the world–a sign of globalization of popular music.

Rio de Janeiro's history is as amazing as its landscape and its women. The first European to see the coast of Brazil was a Spanish mariner, Vicente Yañez Pinsón, who explored the East coast of Brazil in late 1499 and sailed into the Amazon in early 1500. He had accompanied Columbus in his first voyage to America in 1492. When he reached the Amazon River he thought that it was the Ganges. Pedro Alvares Cabral followed in 1500 and established claims to the region for the king of Portugal. Amerigo Vespucci may have also sailed along the Brazilian Coast in 1500. A few years later he participated in another expedition and wrote an account of the "the New World" that became a best seller in Europe.

Rivers of pristine waters run down the high mountains surrounding the well-protected bay. During their expeditions, Portuguese and Spanish sailors were delighted to enjoy fresh mountain water so near the port. In the 16th century, Portuguese ships would leave Europe and stop in Brazil before turning around South Africa's Cape of Good Hope and sailing to India to trade in spices or silk. The ships would return through the same routes, taking a year or two in the process. Rio was strategically placed to help these long transcontinental voyages. Trade winds and the availability of fresh supplies made this stop convenient.

The origin of the name Brazil is somewhat of a mystery but it seems to have derived from the name of attractive red trees that were common in Brazil. In 1520, during his extraordinary trip around the world, Magellan's ships stopped in Rio, and the sailors of the five ships, starved for food and sex after many months at sea, enjoyed fresh water and fresh food and a famous orgy with native women who may have been cannibals. In his book, *Over the Edge of the World*, Lawrence Bergreen gives a fascinating account of Magellan's sixty thousand mile ocean trip, which began in 1519. Bergreen's book recounts Magellans' discovery of the passage between the Atlantic and the Pacific oceans and contains information on the bay of Rio in the 16th Century and Magellan's stop there. The expedition ended in 1521 albeit without Magellan, who was killed in the Philippines.

In 1555, the French made an alliance with the natives to invade the bay and to found their own "France Antartique." Estácio de Sá led the Portuguese in fierce battles against the French, eventually defeating them and building a fortress and the city of Rio on March 1, 1565. However, the area remained a battlefield for the Portuguese. They had to deal with the native Tamoio Indians, who were cannibals. In 1567, Estácio de Sá received a poisoned arrow in his chest and died. In 1710 and 1711, the French tried again unsuccessfully to invade Rio, but Portugal was able to retain control of Rio and of Brazil.

Rio evolved into a gold trading port for the mining region, Minas Gerais. In 1763, Rio became the capital of Brazil, at a time when Brazil was still a Portuguese colony. A few decades later Napoleon invaded Portugal and the Portuguese King, John VI, and the Royal Court went into exile in Rio. In 1808, Rio became the capital of the Portuguese Empire while Portugal was occupied by the French. By that time the Portuguese Empire had colonies on all Continents. Thus in 1808 Rio governed parts of China (Macau), Indonesia (East Timor), Malaysia (Malacca), India (Goa), Africa (Angola, Mozambique, Cape Verde and Guinea Bissau) and Europe (Portugal, Azores, Madeira and Algarve).

After Brazil declared independence in 1822, Rio de Janeiro remained the capital of the only long-term monarchy of the Americas, with King John VI's son, King Peter I (Don Pedro Primero), as the

Emperor. His son Peter II reigned until the fall of the monarchy in 1889. Rio kept its status as the capital of the newfound republic until 1960, when Brasília was officially designated the new capital of Brazil. However, for several years many government offices remained in Rio while Brasília was being built in a relatively undeveloped part of Brazil. Today, Rio is still Brazil's wealthiest state in terms of per capita income, largely due to the oil business. However, the major headquarters of the Brazilian economy are now in São Paulo, a state whose population is almost three times larger than Rio.

During my early visits to Rio de Janeiro in the 1960s, a phenomenon that I found curious was the rapidity with which Copacabana beach would empty itself at a given time of the day. Because Rio is on the East coast of Latin America, and because there are tall buildings along the Avenida Atlantica, which divides the buildings from Copacabana beach, and high mountains immediately behind, when the sun starts going down in the early afternoon, the beach quickly loses its sunshine. This seems to be the signal, to those who are sun-bathing practically naked on the beach, that it is time to go home. Since most live only two to three blocks away from the beach, this makes the trip home easy. To one who comes from far, it is strange to see a beach crowded with literally tens of thousands of people one moment to become practically empty the next.

At that time I was introduced to Brazilian cuisine. I was impressed by a vegetable that I had never seen before, the *palmito*, which is the heart of young palm trees. The *palmito* was often served as a soup, *sopa de palmito*, or cut in small pieces and served with some sauce. At the time I did not like the idea that a young tree had to be destroyed for people to enjoy a meal. I felt a bit like a cannibal, which was strange because I did not feel this way when I ate meat. I was also introduced to *feijoada*, a popular but heavy meal, based on beans and pork, and to grilled *camarões* (large shrimps), which where not common in other parts of the world at that time.

Somehow globalization seems to have reduced the pleasure of finding new foods, a pleasure that still existed three or four decades ago before trade grew. There are now fewer surprises in the world and in some sense this has made it less interesting because it feels as if there is much less to discover. Globalization has widened our choices while reducing our discoveries and our surprises. It is not obvious whether we have gained in the process, although most economists would insist that we have. There may be diminishing returns to choices; more choices may cease to improve welfare after a certain a point. Today's Marco Polo would have far less novel material with which to amaze the folks back home.

Another culinary surprise for me was the *churrascaria*, the typical Brazilian steakhouse. Though this concept does not seem to have an equivalent use elsewhere, it has started to be exported in recent years. A *churrascaria* opened in Washington in 2006 and some exist in other major cities including New York. In these *churrascarias* one pays a fixed price and waiters come to the tables with huge chunks of different types of meat to fill one's plate. The serving continues until the customer gives a signal to stop, at times switching a medallion from green to red. In these circumstances, when the cost of each additional piece of meat is zero, one tends to consume so much meat that the cholesterol level must go up dramatically. I have often wondered whether an increased incidence of heart attacks follows visits to *churrascarias.* I have not seen a survey on this question. In any case, these visits are marvelous sins to be committed occasionally. Being away from home is always a good excuse for committing them because it removes the feeling of guilt that one has when he/she commits these sins at home.

Another characteristic of Rio at that time was its nightlife. There was an infinite number of nightclubs, some small and some very large where famous singers would perform. One such famous singer was Maysa, who had married a member of the Matarazzo family, a rich Italian family with claims to an aristocratic background. Maysa had become Maysa Matarazzo, but the marriage may not have been a happy one. One day, on a crowded afternoon and at the peak of her fame, she parked her car on a high bridge and jumped from it. Her suicide was a very tragic event; Brazil and the world lost a very talented singer.

One night I was sitting in one of these nightclubs with an OAS colleague from Chile, and we started a conversation with a woman and a young girl of perhaps thirteen or fourteen who were sitting at a nearby table. I thought that they might be mother and daughter, although the girl was light skinned and very beautiful, while the woman was darker and average in look. We talked with them for some time while we were having dinner. At the end of the dinner we were getting up to leave when the two women proposed that we go to their apartment nearby. We were taken aback because the girl was really very young. In our naiveté, and because of the apparent differences between the two women, we had not thought of them as prostitutes. When we refused to follow them, they became angry and started arguing that we had wasted their time and had made them miss other opportunities to earn money. This "opportunity cost" argument was one that, as economists, we understood. The end of the story was that we paid them for services *not* rendered, recognizing the economic validity of their argument.

Another noteworthy individual I recall was a shoe-shiner who was a real comedian. He charged more because he would shine your shoes while making music, using his shoe-shining equipment as his instruments. The music was what economists call an externality for which he expected to be paid. I also recall conversations with taxi drivers, who are always a source of interesting insights. One day I started a conversation with a cab driver from the Northeast of Brazil. When I asked him whether or not he liked Rio, he told me that he did not like it much because it was too cold. This comment was directed at a city where one can go outside and swim almost every day of the year. I also recall a conversation, which I report more fully in the chapter on Chile, with a taxi driver on September 4, 1970, the day when Salvador Allende, a left wing politician, was announced to be the newly elected president of Chile. I had asked the taxi driver's reaction to Allende's election and was surprised by the reply. He said: "Senhor, I am a poor man who drives this old taxi for 12 hours a day. But I play the lottery every week. Suppose I win, do you think that it would be fair for the government to take that money away from me?" At this point I concluded that communism would not have a chance in Brazil.

Brazil did face a communist guerilla, reportedly funded by Cuba, in the late 1960s when it had a military government. One of the most spectacular moments of this period was portrayed in the film, *Four Days in September*. In 1969, a group of upper-middle-class youths kidnapped the US Ambassador to Brazil, Charles Elbrick. The youths managed to achieve their goal, to exchange the American Ambassador for communist prisoners through negotiations. One of the prisoners released was José Dirceu. After leaving the jail in Brazil, Dirceu went to Cuba where he received military training. In Cuba, he decided to change his look and identity and to return to Brazil, in order to promote the communist revolution in Latin America's largest country. He underwent plastic surgery and completely changed his facial features. He returned to Brazil with a new face, a new name and fake documents. He started a new life, got married, and had kids in a part of Brazil different from the one he had left in 1969.

When the military dictatorship signed a broad amnesty act in 1979, Dirceu "came out of the cold" and revealed his true identity to his startled family. He then asked for a divorce before returning to Cuba. In Cuba, he again underwent plastic surgery in order to undo the earlier procedure and returned to Brazil as his more or less original self. Twenty-four years later, in 2003 he became President Lula's chief of staff and the main cabinet figure. After thirty-three months as the Government's "team captain" (as Lula had described him) he was impeached on corruption charges and was forced to leave the government. Some believe that he remained active in Brazilian politics, albeit from behind the scenes. Without any shadow of doubt, his life was fascinating and the stuff of movies.

Returning to my conversation with the taxi driver, his words made me think about redistributive policies through taxation. When the government is unhappy with the prevailing distribution of income generated by the private market and by existing property rights and social norms, taxation seems like a logical instrument. The use of taxes to change the income distribution is not a recent invention. I recall the first time that I encountered an argument about redistributive taxation that was popularized by the "public choice school" and by conservative economists. In the past, state power had been used by the aristocracy to extract rents or taxes from the masses. The payment of taxes had often been mostly in kind: shares of crops or direct work, because the taxpayers had little money income. Redistribution had been prevalently from the masses to those at the top, who controlled the government and who had a monopoly over the use of force.

With the introduction of representative and democratic governments, which came into existence mainly in the 20th century, the roles should have changed. The masses, who presumably controlled the democratic governments through their votes, were expected to introduce policies aimed at exploiting the richer classes, thus reversing the historical pattern. There was fear that a democratic system of election, combined with the availability of a progressive income tax (the kind of income tax that became popular especially after World War Two), would lead to high effective tax rates on the rich in order to raise the disposable income of the more numerous poorer masses.

I first read this argument in the classic book, *First Principles of Public Finance* by Antonio De Viti De Marco, a rich and prominent Italian public finance scholar writing more than a century ago. This English edition was published in 1936, but the first Italian edition had been published in 1888. In 1888, elections were still hardly democratic because almost no country had universal representation. Brazil had just abolished slavery. Voters often had to be property owners, and in many countries women could not vote. Furthermore, the modern global income tax had not yet entered the arsenal of tax instruments available to the policymakers. Why is it that full democracy with highly uneven income distributions, and with the availability of the modern global income tax, especially in Latin America. has not led to the exploitation of the rich by the poor, who are clearly in the majority, as predicted by De Viti De Marco? It is not easy to find an answer. One can only speculate.

A possibility is that a society could have an uneven income distribution but is socially mobile so that the composition of those who are rich keeps changing. As a result, many citizens, even when their income is low, may think that one day they will become rich and, at that time, would not want to be faced with highly progressive taxes. In other words there may be a kind of "option demand" for moderate or low rates as an assurance for possible future success. Thus, the more optimistic people are about their future prospects, the less inclined they would be about favoring progressive taxation. Perhaps this is the reason why, as surveys indicate, many (U.S.) Americans think that the normal rate for the income tax should be around twenty five percent. This optimism may explain why surveys in Europe and in the United States often find that income inequality does not seem to have much of an impact on whether or not people are happy. Those with a low income may look toward a future with higher incomes and more happiness. A majority of the individuals with below average incomes expect or hope to have a future income above the mean. It is not likely that the Brazilian society is very mobile. However, what may lead to similar results is that Brazil is a country in which optimism prevails, as shown by the taxi driver's response to my question. The *objective* chance of a poor man striking it rich may be small but as long as he thinks, *subjectively*, that the chance is there, he may not wish to live in an Allende world (should Lady Luck pay a visit). It is perceptions that drive actions, not reality. Of course this taxi driver may have had a personality different from the average.

While in Brazil, one will often hear statements that Brazil is the greatest country in the world, "o maior país do mundo" or that it is the land of the future, "o país do futuro," even though cynics occasionally add that "it will always be." Although hardly recognized as such by the rest of the world, Brazilians may have some reason to believe in their motto. During the whole twentieth century only the economies of a handful of nations (Japan, Taiwan, Korea, Norway, and Finland) grew faster than Brazil. With the exception of Japan, these were all small economies. From 1901 to 2000, the Brazilian economy grew about one hundred times, while its population expanded less than tenfold. From 1920 to 1980, per capita income doubled every couple of decades. In the most recent years, the economy's growth rate has picked up, making some feel that the future may have finally arrived. However, income distribution worsened in the last forty years, and education and infrastructure became persistent causes of concern for the continuation of this growth pattern in the twenty-first century. The income distribution has improved mildly during the Lula administration.

In any case, and returning to the earlier discussion on taxation, I am surprised that income taxes have played such a limited role not only in Brazil but also in all of Latin America, even after the Latin American countries became democratic, most citizens voted, and the income distribution became more unequal. This is an interesting phenomenon to some extent replicated nowadays in the USA. Working class people in conservative U.S. states supported tax cuts and President Bush's overall tax policy. Such policies mostly rewarded higher income individuals. Meanwhile, the income gap between college graduates and blue-collar workers widened in America.

When income taxes were introduced, with nominally high marginal tax rates, it was possible for the rich to either avoid or evade them. Perhaps with the help of economists, the rich have been successful in convincing everyone that progressive income taxes make a country poor so that they should not be tried seriously. This was the main message that accompanied the supply-side revolution of the 1980s. In Latin America, most of the incomes of the truly rich come from returns to capital investments (in the forms of profits, interests, capital gains, dividends, rents and so on), and many of these countries have taxed these incomes at low rates for fear that high rates would lead to capital flight. By doing so, they have exempted from taxation much of the tax base.

In Brazil and in other parts of Latin America, I was struck by the ethnic characteristics of the income distribution. It was rare to find African- Brazilians in significant administrative positions in the Brazilian government. Also walking on the Avenida Atlantica boardwalk, one would often observe women taking care of small children. The children were almost always light-skinned while the women were dark. The women were obviously servants taking care of their employers' children. Still, there seemed to be little open friction or hostility between the races, and one had the impression of a melting pot in a way that one did not have in the US at that time.

Brazil has increasingly become a melting pot. There is a growing mixture of races, but this phenomenon occurs mostly among the lower classes. According to the CIA's *World Fact Book* data, those of European descent represent fifty-five percent of the Brazilian population, five percent have pure African heritage, while forty-five percent are of mixed ancestry, including black, native-American, and Asian. While the elite remains overwhelmingly white, the poor mingle freely, creating an ever-growing percentage of mulattos. On the other hand, the North American working class is barely mixed. In fact in the United States there may be more mixing at the top than at the bottom. Interracial marriages in the United States, while growing in recent years, represent still an almost insignificant proportion of total marriages. Thus a visible distinction between whites and blacks remains in the ethnic landscape of the US.

A March 31, 1964 coup led by the military ran the country until the 1980s, when democratically elected civilian governments returned. For many of those years Delfim Netto was the finance minister and the economic Czar of Brazil. In this period Brazil would experience significant inflation and, at least throughout the 1970s, a very high rate of growth. The Brazilian model of development attracted much attention at that time. Brazilian GDP grew more than five percent every year from 1968 to 1980, and at least nine percent in more than half of those years. These were considered exceptionally good rates; however, inflation was also high. Brazil introduced widespread indexation of wages and prices, a policy that led the famous conservative economist, Milton Friedman, to state that indexation might have removed the pain of inflation. However, while the institution of widespread indexation might have removed the pain of inflation for some groups and sectors, it had also made people more tolerant of inflation. This would become a major problem in later years, especially for poorer people, when the rate of inflation accelerated.

The military leaders wanted growth at any costs so that various highly unorthodox policies were pursued. This seems to be a characteristic of authoritarian governments: to try to legitimize their leaderships with high rates of growth. One of the policies that they pursued was the granting of subsidies to enterprises and sectors not through the budget but through credits from the Banco do Brasil. This bank functioned as a national development bank that could finance spending without approval from Congress. In some ways the Banco do Brasil provided blank checks for ministers who could authorize some expenditures without congressional authorization. These monetary subsidies created a situation whereby the official budget was mostly in balance, suggesting fiscal prudence, while inflation was high. Banco do Brasil was in turn financed by the Central Bank which simply printed money thus leading to inflation. This policy led some foreign economists, including some well-known ones, to believe that the Brazilian experience proved that there was no relation between inflation and fiscal deficits--a topic much discussed at the time.

Another widely used policy was that of tax incentives. This reflected an extremely active, interventionist policy in which the state played a large role in allocating resources and in economic decisions. Obviously the political leaders thought that they were smarter than the market. The government also acted to raise the investment rate and the saving rate in addition to allocating resources geographically and sectorally through tax incentives, in a Brazilian version of industrial policy. One would joke at the time that there was no tax incentive that the Brazilian government did not like. Enormous resources were allocated for the development of the Northeast but with disappointing results. The region continues to be poor to this day.

If Brazil could be named as the original colony of exploitation in the Americas, the Northeast region would be its poster child. For example Bahia, the largest northeastern state, is where Jorge Lopes Bixorda brought the first load of slaves to the Americas in 1538. Captive workers were forced to toil in large sugar cane, tobacco, and cacao plantations until the Lei Aurea, or the "Golden Act," freed all slaves on May 13th 1888. It was almost thirty years after the USA had outlawed slavery and almost sixty years after the English had declared the slave trade illegal. Brazil was the last country in the Western Hemisphere to free the slaves.

After slavery was abolished, several landowners continued treating their newly termed "dependent workers" almost as poorly as before. Because of the large sizes of the farms and the huge distances, the freed slaves often had no alternatives but to continue to work in the same farms where they had worked as slaves. There were different ways to keep workers tied to the land, through debt or indenture. Landowners paid very low wages, controlled voting rights (*voto de cabresto*), and maintained the dependent population in absolute misery and ignorance. These practices persisted elsewhere, but were predominant in the Northeast. Fiscal incentives did not help to make the economy of that region blossom.

However, the granting of so many tax incentives reduced tax revenue and encouraged tax evasion, thus creating some financing difficulties for the military government. In the late 1960s, when the ratio of taxes to GDP was still very low, the military government launched a campaign against tax evasion. Posters went up all over the country, painted black to symbolize the conscience of a tax evader. At one point teams of tax inspectors would descend on parts of towns to inspect the books of shops and to observe the activities of restaurants or free professionals.

This campaign produced a negative reaction among the people, which led the military government to soften its approach and to declare that in the future taxes would be collected "with kindness." It seems that even military governments have to pay attention to popular reactions, as Nicoló Macchiavelli taught the world five hundred years ago in his book *The Prince*.

Because of inflation and the government attempt to fight it, in part through the fixing of the tariffs of public enterprises, and because of the effects of tax incentives and inflation itself on public revenue, public enterprises had very limited resources with which to maintain or upgrade their infrastructure and they could not depend on transfers from the government. At the same time the fast rate of economic growth, combined with low tariffs, increased the demand for services and created serious supply bottlenecks. A genuine "infrastructure gap" developed. The quality of the public services fell dramatically as a result of poor maintenance and lack of investment. This fall affected rich and poor equally. Rich people could not escape the huge bottlenecks in the traffic, the low quality of telephone services, and the blackouts.

An amusing index of this problem was the number of telephones that one would find in government offices. One could determine the rank of a government official by how many telephones there were on his or her desk: the higher the rank, the greater the number of phones. For very high ranks, there could be as many as eight or even twelve phones, all placed in a neat circle on the public official's desk. Often times a secretary's only duty was to successively pick up the various phones in the hope of getting an open line to make a telephone call. Most of the time there would be no line available. In later years the privatization of public utilities would lead to better services and higher prices for the services. The privatization of telecommunications has dramatically improved lives, not only in Brazil but all over the world. In 2007 there were around one hundred million cell phones in Brazil, making it the fourth largest market in the world, after China, Japan, and the US.

In the 1970s a controversy erupted, in part sparked by an article published in *The American Economic Review* by an American economist, Albert Fishlow, about the connection between economic growth and income distribution. Fishlow had argued that the obsession with growth, shown by the Brazilian government, had created a lack of attention to the problem of income distribution. He argued that the distribution of income was getting less even and that growth was largely benefiting the richer income classes and not the majority of the population. The "Gini coefficient," an index of the "fairness" of the income distribution, was not improving, but was pointing toward increasing inequality. There were those who argued then, as they do now, that the distribution of income should be ignored because, over the long run, growth would benefit everyone. Their often- repeated statement was that a high tide lifts all boats.

At that time I had written a paper entitled "Redistributing Income through the Budget in Latin America," illustrating the difficulty of applying the tax system, and especially the expenditure side of the budget, to bring about a better distribution of income. The paper, published in 1974 in the Italian *Quarterly Review* of the Banca Nazionale del Lavoro, went against what many people wanted to believe. The argument was that often public spending ends up helping those from the upper-middle class who deliver the services to the poor, such as school teachers, school administrators, those who work in hospitals and so on rather than those who are intended to benefit. Decades later the conclusions of that paper were rediscovered and given additional empirical and theoretical support by some economists, including Alberto Alesina at Harvard. The argument of whether growth reduces poverty reappeared in full force in recent years, especially in connection with World Bank policies. This proves many economic questions do not change over time as much as the answers to them.

In that period I met several interesting Brazilians and maintained contact with some of them in later years. When I was chair of the economics department at American University, I was fortunate to have as my colleague Celso Furtado, the famous Brazilian economist who had come to Washington around 1970 as a visiting professor at AU. He had been a leader of the so-called "structuralist school," an influential school with strong supporters within the Economic Commission for Latin America (ECLA, or CEPAL in Spanish) in Santiago. The exponents of this school believed that structural obstacles, such as the distribution of land, the dependence of Latin American countries on commodity exports, the peripheral position of these countries in the world economy, the uneven distribution of income, the low tax burden, and other similar factors made it difficult for Latin American countries to develop faster. Thus, they recommended structural policies, such as land and tax reform, to remove some of these obstacles.

One should remember that at that time Latin America was growing at a reasonable rate. However, the poorest deciles were not benefiting much from the growth, especially considering the rapid population growth. The structuralists believed that a more even income distribution would stimulate faster growth by creating larger domestic markets for mass-consumed products. The uneven income distribution concentrated spending power in the hands of the few, causing a small domestic market for these products, which, in the structuralists' view, restrained domestic production. These views conflicted somewhat with the situation in Brazil, which at that time was growing at a high rate in spite of the very uneven income distribution. Some would say that Brazil's growth was actually the result of this uneven distribution since it presumably increased the country's rate of saving. Exponents of the structuralist school had a strong leftist bent that led them to favor more governmental intervention in the economy. Despite our differing points of view, Furtado and I often lunched together at the university and we engaged in lively, but always friendly, discussions. I recall him as a good looking, serious, cultured and distinguished gentleman who reminded me of intellectuals of the past.

Another interesting but more effervescent Brazilian with whom I worked during that period was Gerson da Silva. I met him in his capacity as Director of the Joint Tax Program in Washington, part of the American-financed Alliance for Progress. Though formally supported by three joint international institutions (UN, OAS, and IDB), the program was nested within the OAS. I had first worked for this program in 1962 as an assistant to the then Director, Alvaro Magaña, who later became President of El Salvador. I had worked there in the summer months while I was a graduate student at Harvard. In later years, after I had returned to Washington and was teaching at AU, I continued to work as a consultant for this program until 1973.

Gerson da Silva was officially trained in medicine. However, while he was studying to become a medical doctor, he had worked part time in the Ministry of Finance of Brazil and, hard to believe, he had fallen in love with taxation. To him taxes were the levers that could move the world. While most people think of taxes as instruments that impede efforts and actions, da Silva saw them as effective instruments that can promote particular actions. In this he reflected the official Brazilian view at that time. He believed that with enough tax incentives, almost any economic goal became possible. If taxation were a religion, he was the closest I had ever met to a fundamentalist. It is thus not surprising that after getting a medical degree, he decided to abandon the medical profession and move into the tax field. For him the transition must have been easy because he replaced the human patient with the sick economy and medical treatments with tax instruments such as tax incentives. He also convinced himself that he could do more good for mankind working as a tax expert than as a medical doctor. In some ways he was a true humanitarian.

Gerson da Silva did not have any formal training in economics but he was a very intelligent man with the unconstrained imagination of a four-year old. I read somewhere that a Ph.D. in economics gives one a good filter for ideas but it often kills the imagination because so much of the training consists in seeing why something will not work. Da Silva did not have this problem. He simply did not have any filter. The lack of filter combined with a vivid imagination meant that, like an efficient factory, he was constantly producing new ideas. I became a kind of proxy filter for his ideas. Most of these were not practical, but occasionally some were worthwhile. The problem for me was how to make him see the difference.

One time I tried to shoot down one of his ideas by giving him a book that offered a valid and convincing criticism of that particular idea. A few days later I asked him what he thought of the book. The answer was straight and to the point: "I did not read it and I did not like it." At other times he would gather some of the economists working for the Joint Tax Program around a table and present a new idea. He would then make the "tour de table" to listen to reactions or comments. Often everyone would find faults with his idea. After making the round and letting everyone talk, he would conclude, with total honesty, that since he had *not heard* any negative comments of his idea, he would go ahead with it! He was so involved with taxation, and had such a messianic attitude toward it, that one time he invited several people from the Joint Tax Program office for dinner in his Washington apartment. Before dinner was served, he started talking about his latest tax ideas and became so absorbed by them that he totally forgot to serve the prepared dinner. Once he started, he could talk for hours in an interesting combination of Portuguese and Spanish called Portunhol. People eventually took leave with empty stomachs but with their heads full of tax ideas.

Da Silva organized two big international tax conferences in that period, one in Quito, and one in Mexico City. These conferences had a lasting influence on tax policy in Latin America for successive periods. In particular they promoted the view that taxes should be used not only to raise revenue but also to push the economy in what were claimed to be desirable directions. Thus, in some ways the conferences promoted the idea of tax incentives. I contributed two papers to the Mexican conference in which I tried my best to support the Director's ideas despite my own reservations. Sadly Gerson da Silva died of cancer at a young age. He was a wonderful man and one of a kind.

In different ways, Celso Furtado and Gerson da Silva symbolized the Brazilian country's economic policies for the past half century. Both saw the government as a potentially powerful and beneficial agent that could significantly change the economic landscape. It is perhaps fair to state that both questioned the market's power to bring positive changes without the regulatory action of the state.

CHAPTER 2

BRAZIL: AROUND 1980S

In one of my trips to Rio in the early 1980s I became aware of an issue that some twenty years later would result in an economic paper. This paper would eventually play a role in Italian economic policy and, through the Italian example, may also have influenced the policies of some other European countries. One day I was taking a walk on the Avenida Atlantica, the wide avenue that borders Copacabana beach in Rio de Janeiro. I noticed that among the tall buildings on the Avenida (mostly twenty stories high) there was a two-story building that housed a public, elementary school. This scene might seem unexceptional because one finds such schools everywhere. However, it struck me as an anomaly. First of all, the school's proximity to the beach was likely to distract the children from their school activities. But perhaps more importantly, the land facing the beach, which has very high market value, was being used for an activity that, though socially valuable, could very well be located a couple of blocks away where land is much less expensive and the location less distracting to the students. In short, if the school were not there, a tall building could be built in its place that could be used as a hotel or as an expensive office building. Such a building would generate a high income and contribute to tax revenue. In my mind the use of this land for a school was an obvious misallocation of economic resources.

In the paper that I finally wrote on this issue many years later (co-authored by Tej Prakash), I pointed out that the budget of that school would not reflect the opportunity cost of the use of that land, that is the value that the land could have in the most valuable market use. The public budget and the budget of the school would reflect mostly the cash expenses for teachers, cleaning, and maintenance of the building, expenses that would be the same even if the school had been in another location. I argued that in a proper budgetary classification, the budget of the school ought to reflect the true, market, rental value of that land. If this were done, it would be immediately evident that the land was being misused and that the school, and indirectly the public sector, was using far more resources for educating the children of that school than reflected by its cash budget. Brazil would gain economically if the land on which the school was located was put to its economically most valuable use while the school was moved a couple blocks away from the beach to less expensive premises.

The paper, entitled "The Cost of Government and the Misuse of Public Assets", recognized that this "misuse of public assets" was a common problem and recommended that: (a) public assets should be put to their most productive uses, and (b) if they remained in public uses, the budget of the activities using the assets (education, defense, health, etc.) should reflect the true rental value of these assets. Only in this way would the true cost of various governmental activities be known, and this would create incentives to use these assets more efficiently. This paper was originally issued as a working paper of the IMF and later published in a book *Public Finance in Developing and Transitional Countries*, edited by Jorge Martinez-Vazques and James Alm (Elgar, 2003). This book was in honor of a well-known Canadian economist, Richard Bird.

In 2002, the paper provided some intellectual guidance to the Italian government. The Italian government controlled enormous property that had been generating a very low return due to the "misuse" of many state assets. Many of these assets were used in low value activities. Estimates indicated that the market value of the public assets owned by the Italian state, as a share of the Italian gross GDP, was larger than the Italian public debt and almost three times as large as the value of the assets owned by the British government. In Italy there were many egregious examples of misuse of public assets. My preferred example, cited in the published paper, was the location of the largest Italian jail near the Vatican, in the most expensive area of Rome! I could not avoid thinking what a magnificent hotel or museum that building could accommodate.

Unfortunately, the need to get cash to keep the fiscal deficit below the three percent of GDP prescribed by the Maastricht Treaty of the European Monetary Union soon took precedence over the need to use the public assets more productively. The government started contemplating selling the buildings where the ministries were located to a government controlled institution and then renting them right back. The receipt from the sale would be counted as revenue thus making the fiscal deficit look smaller but nothing else would change. This additional public income could sustain *current* spending. This was the classic case of pushing some accounts off budget. This operation of financial engineering would not bring the public assets to better economic uses. Learning from the Italians, other European countries started considering similar operations. Thus a paper intended to increase efficiency may have resulted in a lowering of the net worth of the public sectors, without clearly improving the efficiency in the use of resources. However, the attempt to get a higher return to public assets has been evident in some other countries. In Istanbul, a large public jail has become a luxury hotel, and in India a recent policy will move city jails outside the cities and sell the land where they had been located for high profits. In Argentina in the 1990s, the old storage buildings along the river Plate, that had been abandoned for decades and had been invaded by rats, became the site of the most chic area of Buenos Aires (Puerto Madero). In Tokyo, the buildings that had been used by the national railroad became the sites of very modern offices and convention centers after that railroad was privatized. Privatization removes legal constraints and makes these changes possible.

In 1974, I joined the IMF as head of the Tax Policy Division and, after a two-year period of leave from my university position, I decided to remain at the IMF and resign from my tenured position as Professor of Economics at American University. As a full professor and a well-paid consultant to the OAS, the World Bank and other institutions, I had been earning a high income so the decision had not been easy on purely financial grounds. Also at that time, after the breakdown of the Bretton Woods agreement, the IMF was not going through one of its most glorious periods. My income fell somewhat when I joined the IMF, probably not a usual experience for those joining the Fund. Between 1974 and 2000, when I left the IMF, my involvement with Brazil was always somehow connected with Fund activities. During my twenty-seven years at the Fund, first as a Division Chief and then, starting in 1981, as Director of the Fiscal Affairs Department, I continued to visit Brazil from time to time for a variety of reasons: to assess the fiscal performance, to provide advise on public finance matters, and to participate in conferences.

During one of these visits, someone approached a colleague from the Fund outside our hotel and offered to sell him some presumably precious stones. As is well known, Brazil produces many nice semi-precious stones. My colleague seemed interested and there followed a prolonged negotiation that resulted in a final transaction. He bought a nice looking stone. Like buying an old car (a "lemon"), the classic economic example that earned George Akerlof the Nobel Prize in economics in 2001, this was the kind of transaction in which only one side has all the information. That information, of course, was whether or not the stone was a fake. I would never buy a precious stone in this way. I was thus surprised when my colleague, who was a smart man, did not show any particular concern about whether or not the stones were genuine. He seemed to be only concerned with the price. When I questioned him later, he explained that he had paid relatively little for the stone and would have it mounted into a beautiful ring for his wife before leaving Brazil. He admitted that the stone was probably a fake. But he had paid only a small fraction of what he would have paid if the stone had been authentic. He added that it did not matter whether the stone was a fake or not because it was still very attractive and, once it was mounted into a beautiful ring, his wife would assume that the stone was authentic and she would love it. She would have no reason to question its authenticity. Whether the stone was a fake or not would not matter. Economists would say that the wife's welfare would be greatly enhanced by the gift while my colleague's welfare would also be enhanced because his purse had been little affected while getting the benefit of making his wife happy.

This was an example of situations in which a lie, combined with what economists call "asymmetric information", can increase welfare! It reminded me of a story that an Indian Professor from the University of Leicester once told me. He said that occasionally he had people over for dinner. At the time when he would serve tea, he would ask people how they liked it. Some wanted a full spoon of sugar, some a half spoon, some a quarter spoon, some a sweetener. When the tea was ready to be served, he would put half a spoonful in all cups and then distribute the tea as if he had followed precisely their requests. Nobody ever complained or seem to notice the difference. It is not clear whether they ever realized that their instructions had not been followed. Thus, again, the use of asymmetric information can lead to beneficial results and can simplify some tasks.

However, asymmetric information can be also costly, as Akerlof's used- car example showed in his discussion of buying "lemons." The short story, "The Necklace," by Guy de Maupassant, the famous 19th century French writer, makes that point strikingly clear. It is the tale of an attractive French lady who is married to a lower-level functionary working in a French ministry. One day the husband receives an invitation for both of them to attend the annual ministerial ball, one of the distinctive social events in Paris. This is a great honor for the couple and the opportunity of a lifetime. However, the wife becomes immediately concerned that she has neither the proper clothes for the occasion nor the jewels to wear, as required by the etiquette of the time. They invest their meager savings in buying a proper dress, but there remains the problem of the jewels. She cannot possibly go to a ministerial ball, attended by the most important people of Paris, without wearing some beautiful jewel. Fortunately she has a friend, married to a rich man, who always wears beautiful jewels. Thus, somewhat embarrassed, she asks her friend to lend her one of her jewels. The friend immediately agrees and lends her a stunningly beautiful necklace. The couple goes to the ball, where the wife is much admired and is even invited to dance by the Minister. They both have the most wonderful evening of their lives.

When they return to their modest apartment, tired but happy, they discover to their horror that the wife no longer has the necklace around her neck. A frantic search for the necklace proves unsuccessful. The couple is devastated. What can they do? The only solution is for them to search the next day, in the many jewelry shops of Paris, for a necklace that looks exactly like the lost one and hope that the friend will not notice the difference. After a long search, they finally find a match. However, the price is well beyond their modest means. They sell whatever objects of value they have to a pawnshop and negotiate a huge loan at usury rates. They return the necklace to the friend, and the sad process of repaying the huge debt begins. The wife is forced to get menial jobs which are tiring and below her status as the wife of an employee of a ministry. She has to work more and more hours and her health deteriorates. Within a relatively short time she starts to age rapidly. The couple is forced to cut all their social relations and move to a more modest apartment. The wife has not seen her friend since she returned the necklace, but one day she runs into her by chance. They greet each other and the friend is shocked by how much the lady has aged. She asks her whether she has been ill. At this point the lady who had lost the necklace decides to tell her friend what happened. The friend is shocked by the story and immediately reveals that the necklace had been a fake of little monetary value. Obviously asymmetric information can have different consequences depending on the circumstances.

In the 1970s, Rio was still a relatively safe city and one could walk around Copacabana at night without much concern. The major problem was the number of ladies of the night who would approach individuals, especially those who looked foreigners. At that time, a story circulated around the IMF which I can recall, although I cannot vouch for its truthfulness. The story goes that one of the Fund missions to Brazil had been led by a distinguished looking European gentleman who, in the evening, after a full day's work, liked to go alone to eat in a good restaurant. The first night he walked out of the hotel an attractive girl solicited him. When he asked the price, she told him that it would cost $100, of course 1970 prices. He replied that it was well above the IMF allowance for daily expenses, and therefore no deal was made. The following night he again went out alone and was again approached by the same girl who was more elegantly dressed and prettier than the night before. He once again asked the price and was told $100. He offered $30 but the girl turned him down. This scene repeated itself for several nights during which the girl was becoming progressively more beautiful. However, her asking price had remained $100. The man's offering price increased slightly, but only to $40. Supply and demand had not met so no deal was struck and no transaction had taken place.

On the weekend, using an IMF program that financed a spouse trip after the working spouse had spent two hundred nights away from home, the gentleman's wife joined him from Washington and in the evening they both got dressed to go out for dinner. When they left the hotel, he took another direction from that of previous nights so as not to run into the girl. However, after a short walk he saw that the girl was walking straight in their direction. She was more beautiful than ever. He covered his face with his hand pretending not to see her and hoping that she would not say anything. The girl ignored the couple. He was much relieved when she passed them without even looking or saying anything. But once she was a few steps behind them, she stopped and spoke loud enough for him to hear; she said, "Now you see what you get for $40!" As I said, I cannot vouch for the truthfulness of this story.

With the passing of the years the high growth rate of the 1970s slowed down, the crime rate went up, and the inflation rate went up sharply. If there had been a "misery index," measuring the inflation rate and the crime rate combined, it would have gone through the roof. By the mid 1980s Rio had become a dangerous place and, as a consequence, had lost some of its charm. By this time all the federal public administration had moved to Brasília, the military were no longer in power, a left-leaning administration was in control of Rio, and tourism had fallen dramatically. Rio had lost its claim as a preferred destination of jet-setters. Because Rio was no longer the capital of Brazil, my official trips to Brazil took me to the new capital, with the exception of occasional conference related trips to Rio or San Paulo. The routine missions of the IMF were almost always limited to the capital city of a country because the IMF dealt only with national governments.

In August 1989, on the way to a mission to Argentina, I stopped in Rio to participate in a conference organized by Rudi Dornbusch, a prominent German economist teaching at MIT who was then married to Eliana Cardozo, a Brazilian economist. The conference was a good one attended by several well-known Brazilian and foreign economists. By that time inflation had become the major problem in Brazil, and therefore much of the discussion pertained to addressing and coping with it. There was much less talk about inflation without pain, although indexation had become widespread. Two episodes connected with this trip are worth reporting. The first was the purchase of some naïf paintings and the second concerned my family's stopover in Rio.

By 1989, Rio had become so dangerous that we were advised not to walk far from the hotel even though it was right in the middle of Copacabana. After the conference a few of us took a walk on the crowded Avenida Atlantica. I was particularly interested in looking at the many paintings that were being sold right on the street. We stopped by an elderly lady who was selling some of her naïf paintings. Her name was Nelita Bessa, and her paintings reflected the kind of charming detail that is often typical of women naïf painters. They were mostly scenes of rural activities such as the picking of cotton or coffee. I asked the price of one painting and was quoted an almost ridiculously low price; the frame alone would have cost much more in Washington. So I asked her how much she would charge for the whole lot of nine paintings that she had, most of which were small. She seemed troubled by the question but she gave me an answer. The total price was so low that I could not resist buying all nine. To this day I still admire the simplicity, charm, composition, and choice of colors that make these paintings striking. Over the years some of them have made their way into my children's (now adult married men) houses.

While the artist was packing up my paintings, I had the distinct impression that she was slightly saddened by the transaction. However, the unhappiness did not seem to come from the price at which she had sold the paintings. One reason may have been that once she had sold the whole lot, she could no longer justifiably hold her spot on the Avenida. I noted that the space she had occupied was next to an elderly gentleman who seemed to be her close friend and who still had many of his paintings for sale. Unfortunately, the man's paintings were modernistic ones that did not have any attraction for me. Perhaps my distaste for his paintings was all the better for me because for the remainder of my trip I would have the problem of carrying all my purchases. This was part of the cost of collecting globally. Incidentally on a trip to Rio in March 2008 I tried to trace the painter without success. I was told that she had retired.

After attending the conference in Rio, my trip would continue to Buenos Aires. Since I was to remain in Buenos Aires for three weeks, I had made arrangements for my wife and two of our sons to join me there toward the end of my mission. We had planned to go to visit the Iguaçu Falls at the corner of Argentina, Brazil, and Paraguay. However, because they had never seen Rio, and Rio was on the way, I had made arrangements for them to stop there for a couple days to see the city. I had warned them about the security problem in Rio and advised them to take only official tours. A couple of weeks later they arrived in Rio and registered at a hotel in front of Copacabana beach, where I had made reservations for them. After a short rest, they decided to walk to the beach in front of the hotel. It was already late afternoon, and the beach was empty so they felt safe. It was still daytime and they were on the beach just in front of the hotel.

They sat on the sand and were enjoying the spectacular sights that Rio has to offer. At a given moment they spotted four young men who seemed to be jogging and moving in their direction. When these boys approached my wife, one of them asked her for the time. At that point my wife felt that something was wrong. Before she realized what was going on, one of the boys had jumped on her trying to snatch her purse, two had jumped on my younger son who was sixteen at the time, and the last one was menacing my older son, who was eighteen, with a broken bottle. My wife had fallen on the sand holding her purse under her while the guy on top of her was trying to get the purse.

At that time my older son, Alex, was a star player on his high school football team; he weighed more than two hundred twenty pounds and had won several international weight lifting competitions. With the shoes that he had in his hands he went after the guy with the broken bottle and hit him hard on the head, knocking him down. After that he hit the guy holding my wife. Within seconds, the attackers started retreating, the ones who had been knocked down doing so with some difficulty. My wife's purse contained their passports, plane tickets, credit cards, and some cash. She had not obeyed the basic rule that in part earned James Tobin the Nobel Prize in economics: one should not put all her eggs in one basket. It is easy to imagine the difficulties my family would have faced if the men had managed to steal my wife's purse. My family told me that once they got back to the hotel, they remained there for the rest of their stay since they were afraid to step out. Thus they missed their chance to see Rio.

When they arrived in Buenos Aires, my family exchanged their story with other conference attendees who had also stopped in Rio on their way from Europe or the US. It was then that they realized how lucky they had been that their attackers did not have real weapons. In one case one of the participants from Holland had been robbed at gunpoint in a crowded bus without any of the people in the bus being able or willing to help. Young men who moved in groups perpetrated these crimes that occasionally resulted in tragic outcomes. The police, too, seemed to be unable or unwilling to do anything. The attitude was that this was a form of income redistribution and that society was partly responsible for it by tolerating wide income disparities. When legal means of redistribution are not available or do not work well, illegal means often come into existence.

The leftist administrations that controlled Rio after the military had left the government seemed largely indifferent to these developments. As one would expect, the murder rate went up sharply and the quality of life, at least for the middle classes, went down dramatically. Street crimes were not the only ones to worry about. Stories began circulating that foreigners were adopting young children, often from the many who lived in the streets, for use of their organs. A Brazilian movie, *Central Station*, deals with this theme. Death squads, perhaps made up of groups of policemen, from time to time took justice in their hands, and summarily executed presumed criminals and street kids. Thus within a few years, Rio went from a place to visit to a place to avoid.

In 1988 a new constitution was approved. Somewhat like a Christmas tree, it was a chance for senators to get everything they wanted. In Brazil, as in the United States, senators represent the states and not the population. Therefore, the small states are over-represented in the Senate. The new constitution created a lot of earmarking of tax revenue. This meant that revenue from particular taxes or from total taxes was assigned legally for specific purposes regardless of the expected growth, over time, of the specific tax. This tied the hands of the national government and made economic policy difficult. In Brazil the constitution became largely a tax constitution and a constitutional lawyer became largely a tax lawyer.

By the late 1980s, Brazil's galloping inflation was fast changing into hyperinflation. Economic policy had become a mess and the rate of turnover for ministers of finance was also inflationary. Four ministers had occupied the post in a few months. A joke circulated at the time that the streets of the major Brazilian cities were becoming dangerous not so much because of crime but because one caught there might be made minister of finance! Public spending and the level of taxation started going up at a record rate. Soon Brazil would no longer be a low-taxed country.

In February 1992, I led a Fund tax mission to Brazil. The government had requested the mission, and we were sent to Brasília for two weeks to study the Brazilian tax system and hold discussions with tax experts and other government officials. We would then write a preliminary report to be presented to the Minister of Finance before the mission returned to Washington. The final report would be sent later from Washington. These tax missions were generally work marathons in which fifteen hour workdays were normal over two-three week periods. This was a particularly strong and unusually large mission including experts from five countries with considerable experience in taxation. It was the first time that I had visited Brasília. Parthasarathi (Partho) Shome, a colleague from the Fund and a very experienced and able Indian economist with a PhD. in economics from a leading American university, accompanied me. By the time the mission left Brasilia it had completed a 170 page report making recommendations for a total reform of the Brazilian tax system.

The idea of building a new capital located more centrally within the country went back at least half a century. In 1955, President Juscelino Kubitschek, a Czech-descent medical doctor, was elected with the slogan "fifty years of progress in five." On October 1, 1957, he signed the law that authorized the building of Brasília, and construction started in early 1960. The chosen site was presumably based on a dream that Don Bosco, the Italian saint who had created the Salesian Order of monks, had had a century earlier. In his dream, Don Bosco had identified the precise coordinates of the new important city. Actually because of debate in parliament, as to where the new capital should be located, Kubitschek may have used Don Bosco's dream to place the capital where he wanted. The building of the city would bring great benefits to those who had owned land in the chosen area, which inevitably brought up questions of corruption.

The main project manager for the new city was Lucio Costa, officially described as an "urbanist" or city planner, and the main architect was Oscar Niemeyer. Niemeyer was a very talented, internationally known, leftist architect who was intrigued by the possibility of creating a functional, planned city from scratch. It should be noted that the issue of whether planning makes for a better city has been hotly debated by sociologists and political scientists. The area where the city was to be built was very dry with humidity indices well below normal. To increase the humidity index, a large artificial lake was created near the city. The surface of the lake was made to be exactly 1000 meters above sea level. The first official building in Brasília was the Don Bosco Shrine designed by Niemeyer.

Being a new, planned city, Brasília has some of the characteristics of other planned cities: it is comfortable but somewhat boring. It has nice weather with temperatures that vary throughout the year between 50 and 90 degrees Fahrenheit, but it remains very dry in spite of the lake. Given Niemeyer's remarkable talent, there are several stunningly beautiful buildings, such as the Ministry of Foreign Affairs (the Palacio Itamaraty), the Cathedral, Congress and a few other buildings. However, Brasília is not a city for pedestrians. Commuting by car is so easy and walking so difficult that many public employees who live in Brasília itself drive home for lunch. But many now live in suburbs that have sprung up outside of the federal district. The new city has attracted a lot of immigrants from other areas. The planning enthusiasm of Niemeyer led him to aggregate similar activities in specific areas. For example, if one wishes to buy shoes, there is a sector where all the shoe shops are located. The same goes for other activities such as hotels, restaurants and supermarkets. The hotels are placed in two sections, the North and the South sections. Niemeyer, who is now over 100 years old, is still active and is engaged in building a large office for the public administration of the state of Minas Gerais in Belo Horizonte.

At the time of the tax mission the Minister of Economy was Marcilio Marques Moreira, a pleasant and able gentleman from a family of diplomats who had been the Brazilian Ambassador to Washington. Minister Marques Moreira facilitated the mission and showed a great deal of interest in its work. Some of the major recommendations of our report had been directed at alleviating the tax wars among the Brazilian states. Unfortunately, the deteriorating economic situation and the impeachment of President Collor for corruption soon after the mission created a situation in which a major tax reform, always difficult in Brazil because of the great power of the states and the restrictions imposed by the Constitution, became impossible. Thus, the report did not have the follow up that we had believed it merited.

Fernando Collor had been the first democratically elected president of Brazil in almost forty years, after the military dictatorship. A relatively unknown figure from the smaller state of Alagoas he became famous as a politician trying to reduce public officials' high wages. The media called these public officials "Maharajas," and Collor was nicknamed "The Maharaja Hunter." He won a presidential race against Lula in 1989 and took power on March 15, 1990. On the 16th he declared a general freeze on all bank accounts in an attempt to control inflation following a plan drafted by leftist economist, Zélia Cardoso de Mello. As one could have anticipated, this plan brought fury to the middle-class and to the population in general. After that precarious start, Collor began to open the economy by reducing import tariffs and lifting trade barriers. Until that time Brazil had been one of the most closed economies in the world. Because Brazil is so large, it has probably suffered less from being closed than smaller economies.

Commercial and industrial associations in São Paulo were profoundly disenchanted with their candidate, and so was the media. They saw this opening as a negative sum game for Brazil, posing a great threat to its industry which had been operating behind high protective walls. In September 1992, thirty months after assuming the presidency, Collor was impeached on corruption charges. His critics pointed to the fact that he was able to unify long-term foes on a common cause: to disrupt the Collor presidency. Later on, the Supreme Court concluded that he had not committed any wrongdoing, but it was too late. The public employees had enjoyed their victory and public spending continued its climb.

While working on the tax report we ran into one of the frequent problems that characterized this kind of work, namely the competition from what I have called "the magic solutions to tax problems." I had run into this problem before in other places, including Argentina. There was always someone, often not a true expert in taxation, proposing some simple reform that would painlessly solve the revenue problem in one swoop. This time the competition came from the "Imposto Unico Sobre Transações" (IUT), a single tax on transactions. A paper by a Brazilian economist had proposed a tax to replace all other taxes. This was presented as a "new tax philosophy." The tax would be a two percent tax rate on all financial transactions and was claimed to produce revenue comparable with the total revenue from the existing taxes at that time. The paper also claimed that this would happen with low compliance costs and low welfare costs.

When paying taxes, taxpayers often face high compliance costs, which are the costs to comply with all tax obligations (i.e. paying tax lawyers, accountants, keeping records, reporting requirements, etc.). Some observers at that time estimated compliance costs in Brazil to range from three to seven percent of GDP, larger than in most other countries. These costs probably went up in later years because of the increasing weight and complexity of the tax system. In recent years, the Brazilian tax system was rated to be one of the most complex systems in the world by both the International Finance Corporation (at the World Bank) and by the *Global Competitiveness Report* of the World Economic Forum. At that time the Imposto Unico had become a popular option. It was also highly popular with members of the Brazilian Congress, with fifty-eight percent reported to support the tax. It was so popular that there had been large street demonstrations *in favor* of this tax!

Over the years there have been occasional proposals in favor of single taxes to replace all other taxes. Many years ago Edgar Feige, a professor of economics at the University of Wisconsin, wrote a paper advocating a tax on all transactions. Examples of such taxes in the form of "turnover taxes" had existed in Europe before the value added tax (VAT) replaced them. Experts normally considered these turnover taxes as highly distortionary and, to be sure, their contribution to revenue was not particularly high. Because of their cumulative or cascading effects, they led to the vertical integration of enterprises thus stifling competition. It was in part for these reasons that the European countries replaced them with VATs. In Argentina in the early 1990, Aldo Dadone, an Argentine economist who later became the President of the Banco de la Nacion, had also proposed a single tax on transactions that would make possible the elimination of all existing taxes. In the United States, a congressman and a talk show host recently proposed a single retail tax to replace all federal taxes and to dispense with the need to have an Internal Revenue System. Their book briefly made the bestseller list, and a bill proposing the change was put before the American Congress. In the run-up to the 2008 elections, a Republican presidential candidate endorsed the proposal.

It seems that, like the search for Eldorado, the search for the painless tax has been a constant dream in Latin America and elsewhere. I myself have been dreaming of a single tax on energy. There may come a day, if technological developments do not help, when a single and perhaps even progressive tax on all energy use might prove desirable. Another recent dream tax has been a tax on checks, which would mean that every time a check is cashed, the bank would retain a small part of the payment. This is a kind of "honey bee" approach to taxation. It is assumed that the taxpayer will not notice the small tax bite. In some way it is a kind of "Tobin tax," although it is applied to domestic transactions. Professor James Tobin, a Nobel prize winner in economics, had proposed a tax on transactions that involved changes from one currency to another to discourage currency speculation. The tax on checks spread like wildfire in Latin America in recent years because it generated some short-run, easy revenue and because directors of taxation liked it. It also gave tax directors some important information on taxpayers' transactions, especially when laws (such as bank secrecy) prevented them from accessing the bank accounts of taxpayers. This bad idea has landed in other continents.

During the last years I spent at the IMF I tried to stop the spread of this tax because I considered it a damaging one, but I was not successful. Countries such as Argentina, Brazil, Colombia, and Peru eventually adopted it. However, I did play a role in preventing its introduction in Mexico in the late 1990s. The president of Colombia had almost convinced Mexican president Ernesto Zedillo to adopt what he was told would be a "painless tax," a miracle tax among all taxes. At that time, Agustin Carstens, the then Vice Minister of Economy, invited me to Mexico. Agustin Carstens would later become a deputy-managing director at the IMF and, in 2006, minister of finance of Mexico. I spent a couple of days with the technical people from the Ministry of Finance and the Central Bank going over the potential costs of this tax. We concluded that it was a bad tax and prepared a note convincing President Zedillo that it would be a mistake for Mexico to adopt it. In 2003, I attended a dinner given by Mr. Enrique Iglesias, then the President of the Inter-American Development Bank, in honor of former President Zedillo. During this dinner, Zedillo was gracious enough to remind me of the good advice that the team had given him.

While I may take some pride for having contributed to the *non*-introduction of the tax on financial transactions (the tax on checks) in Mexico, I may be less proud for having contributed in some marginal way to the non-introduction of the value added tax in the United States. As a result, the US is the only country among the OECD members without a VAT. Given its fiscal situation it would be good if it had it. In 1985-86 I was part of an informal advisory group that provided tax advice to the Ways and Means Committee of the U.S. House of Representatives. This project was part of the Reagan administration's preparation for its fundamental 1986 tax reform. John Makin, an economist with the American Enterprise Institute, a conservative Think Tank in Washington, coordinated the group that included some of the leading public finance economists in the United States. The advisory group met a few times with the members of the Ways and Means Committee, whose powerful chairman at the time was Dan Rostenkowski. At one of these meetings, held at Cape Canaveral in Florida, I was asked to prepare a statement on the VAT and on its potential for use in the USA. The VAT would enable a major reduction in income tax rates, an objective much desired by the supply-siders in the Reagan administration, and would permit an increase in the personal exemption so that millions of low income taxpayers would no longer need to file a tax return. I endorsed this tax because of some of its characteristics, but pointed out that its introduction would inevitably require a large increase, perhaps thirty thousand more, in the personnel of the Internal Revenue System. The IRS had no expertise in this tax and already had its hands full administering the other taxes that it collected. This detail was enough to make the congressmen lose whatever small interest they might have had in this tax. After that meeting, the Hon. Rostenkowski told me a couple of times, half jokingly, that I had killed the VAT in the United States.

At the time of the Brazilian tax mission, the growing fiscal cost of pensions in Brazil was a major concern. Many people, especially civil servants within the national and state governments and military personnel were retiring at young ages with very high pensions that were tied to their last salary. Often times they would be promoted just before retiring so that they could have a higher pension. Many of us thought that a major reform would be necessary to reduce the cost of pensions and to bring some equilibrium to the fiscal accounts. Some of the experts in the Ministry of Economy thought that it might be useful for me to visit the Minister of Labor to discuss the issue. I might be able to elicit a request from him for a Fund mission to analyze future pension developments and recommend some reforms. They arranged a meeting with the minister that pleased some of the Minister's close assistants. These assistants were worried about the budgetary situation and the dynamic of pension spending.

When the Minister received me at his office, he remained seated behind his desk. He made no attempt to move to a sofa or to a table where these informal meetings normally took place. This was unusual vis-à-vis a senior employee of the Fund. I introduced myself and tried to start a conversation with him on the pension problem in Brazil, but there was no reaction. He simply remained silent. I tried to make some more general conversation but, again, there was no reaction. I finally asked him whether there was something the IMF could do to help. He simply answered "nada," none. That was the end of the conversation and of the meeting. The ratio of words spoken to minutes passed must have been very low. It was surely one of the strangest and shortest meetings I had had in my Fund career.

Pensions would become a progressively bigger problem in Brazil, where many public servants would retire at a young age with pensions equivalent to their last monthly salary. The pensions were indexed to wages so that any wage adjustment had an immediate effect on the fiscal cost of the pensions. Wages were indexed for inflation and the courts often played a role in forcing increases in wages for some groups. These increases were then generalized to other groups. If there is such a thing as a pension time bomb, Brazil had it. By the year 2002, Brazil was spending almost eleven percent of GDP for pensions, more than three percent of GDP *above* the OECD average. It appears that the "Maharajas" are still enjoying generous full pension benefits in Latin America's largest country. The cost of pensions has raised the level of total public spending in Brazil to European levels. The level of taxation has followed that of public spending, and Brazil has become the highest taxed developing country or emerging market.

During some of these early trips to Brazil I learned about the Brazilian experiment with the production of ethanol, an alcohol extracted from sugar cane that could be mixed with gasoline thus reducing the need for Brazil to import petroleum. Many cars in Brazil were using it. At that time Brazil did not produce petroleum and therefore had to import what it consumed. I was somewhat skeptical about this economic experiment with ethanol. However, in later years this would prove to have been a very wise investment that, together with later discoveries of oil in the continental shelf off the Atlantic Coast, would make Brazil largely independent from oil import. Among other developments, this has been important in raising the political and economic status of Brazil. Having become one of the BRIC countries, with Russia, India and China, Brazil has moved toward a politically more influential future. I expect that it will become progressively more self-assured and in the process to counter balance the weight of the United States in the Americas.

Returning to Washington after the tax mission in Brasília, my colleague Partho Shome and I had made arrangements to stop in Manaus to have a look at the Amazon River. There we rented a boat and hired a local guide who could tell us something about the river. Manaus became very rich around 1900 during the rubber boom that was largely connected with the growing demand for rubber by the new car industry. In 1897 Manaus felt so rich as to build an opera house, the Teatro Amazonas, a small but beautiful theater that attracted some famous singers. However, since people traveled by boat at that time, Manaus was just too far to bring all the components of an opera. It is over nine hundred miles from the Atlantic coast, although large boats can navigate the Amazon River to reach it. Not far from Manaus, the Rio Negro joins the Amazon River to form a single body of water. This is referred to as the "meeting of the rivers." During our boat ride we observed this "meeting." Because of the different colors of the waters in the two rivers, one can observe the waters from the two rivers moving in parallel for miles without the waters actually mixing. We spent a day going down the river, admiring the many small children swimming like fish in the river near their houses. We also observed that in these villages, the houses were raised on stilts in order to accommodate the river's changing water levels.

We stopped at a small house along the river that served as a mini supermarket. We went into the small room where there were two women, one of whom was the owner, the other a customer. Various live animals, including several kinds of birds, crowded the room, and in the middle was a man who appeared to be entertaining himself with a rather large snake. The two ladies were looking on and seemed amused by the scene. I do not feel comfortable in the presence of snakes so I kept my distance. However, I took advantage of the scene and shot a rather nice photo of this other-worldly scene with the man, the snake, and the smiling women.

Further down the river, we stopped to get out of the boat and walk for a while in the rain forest. I had read so much about the rain forest that I was very curious about the experience of walking through it at least for a while. However, we soon discovered that the ground was very soft and we were not wearing the proper shoes that would have allowed us to walk in the forest. Therefore, we had no other option but to return to the boat and continue our observation from it. Along the river we could observe areas where the trees had been burned to create space for agriculture. The forest was clearly losing its competition against development.

There is some historical evidence that when the Europeans first arrived in the Americas, the Amazon River was populated by many tribes. The indigenous people living there had developed a more integrated style of living, one that allowed them to live in harmony with the surroundings. They had developed immunities to the illnesses that seem to afflict non-indigenous people who venture into the Amazon and had learned how to extract a good living from the forest. According to some historical records, the people who lived there were tall, healthy, and numerous. Furthermore, from the artifacts collected in recent years, researchers have concluded that the people who had lived there had reached a good level of cultural and economic development. However, they suffered a great deal from their encounters with the Europeans.

The sixteenth-century belief in *Eldorados*, or empires of gold within the Amazon, gave rise to many Spanish and Portuguese expeditions, including a disastrous one by Gonzalo Pizarro, the younger brother of Francisco Pizarro, the conqueror of Peru. While the Spaniards entered the Amazon from the West (from Peru and Ecuador), the Portuguese pushed from the East. Over the long run, the Portuguese were more successful, but the indigenous populations suffered from the aggression, exploitation and imported diseases against which they did not have immunities. Many of them were exploited as slaves of the European masters.

Today about twelve percent of Brazil is allocated to indigenous people, and the exploitation of the Amazon continues with potentially disastrous consequences for the world. The forests of the Amazon basin, one of the true lungs of the world, are being progressively destroyed with inevitable implications for global warming. Two fascinating books on the story of the Amazon have been published recently: *Tree of Rivers: The Story of the Amazon*, by John Hemming, and *The Lost City of Z: A Tale of Deadly Obsession in the Amazon*, by David Grann. Both of these books make it clear that the Amazon Basin is more than "a green hell" but a place with a considerable but still not fully known history.

The increasing prices of commodities in recent years, the building of roads though the forest, and the growth of the Brazilian population have created strong economic incentives to exploit the huge area that makes up the Amazon basin. The forests are being destroyed at a rapid rate. An important question is whether the rest of the world should compensate Brazil for *not* exploiting the Amazon. If the forests create an important, positive externality to the whole world, it would appear justified for the world to compensate Brazil for keeping the Amazon in its natural state. How to achieve this is likely to become one of the key questions in future years.

CHAPTER 3

BRAZIL: LIVING WITH HIGH INFLATION IN THE 1990S

By 1993 the rate of inflation in Brazil ranged between twenty-five and thirty-five percent *per month*. It reached 2,780.6 percent over the course of the year. These rates brought on many strange developments. For example, bank robbers were forced to dispose of their loot quickly in order to contain the rapidly decreasing value of the stolen money. This increased their chances of getting caught. Furthermore, gangs that kidnapped people started asking for their ransom in dollars, and bribes also had to be paid in dollars. For a while, new Volkswagens were bought and stored in people's backyards as a way for them to maintain the value of their wealth. Stamps disappeared because their value would have to be changed too frequently making the process very expensive. To mail a letter one had to go to the post office and use stamp machines, which were indexed daily to the change in prices. At the airport shopping carts were outfitted with calculators to enable the adjustment and conversion from one currency to another or from past to present prices. Restaurants no longer printed menus because prices would need to be changed daily. Brazilians had several credit cards and they knew the day when each card would debit their accounts. So, on any given day the choice of which card to use depended on when the card would be debited. Budgeting, for both the government and the private enterprises, became a nightmare. The budgets were often prepared in dollars.

Finally, for a while there were three Brazilian currencies in circulation *at the same time*: the Cruzeiro, the New Cruzeiro and the Cruzado. The relationship between a unit of one currency to the next was one to one thousand. Thus, it took one million units of the oldest currency to make up for one unit of the new currency. Most times when a new currency was introduced, it lost three zeros. This made the situation very confusing especially for foreigners who had great difficulties in distinguishing among the currencies that were still in circulation. On July 25, 1993, the *New York Times* reported: "Since 1980, Brazil has had 4 currencies, 5 wage and price freezes, 9 economic stabilization programs, 11 inflation indexes, 12 finance ministers, and an accumulated inflation rate of 146 billion percent. Without the currency changes, a cup of coffee that sold in 1980 for 15 cruzeiros would sell today for 22 billion cruzeiros."

In September 1993, Delfim Netto, the former, powerful Minister of Finance during the military regime, invited me to São Paulo for an International Symposium on Fiscal Reform. Well-known economists with a specialization in public finance attended the conference. The foreign participants were lodged in a Venetian-style hotel, Ca d' Oro. The first morning we were introduced to the Brazilian fiscal situation. The level of taxation at that time was twenty-four percent of GDP; that of public spending was thirty-three percent of GDP; the inflation rate was more than thirty percent per month. In the period immediately after 1993 these percentages would go up sharply.

There was a lot of discussion of Brazil's tax on financial transactions. It was reported that the revenue from this tax was down which did not surprise most participants at the symposium. Many expected that, with the passing of time, individuals and enterprises would find ways to evade this tax. Professor Arnold Harberger, a well-known economist who had taught at the University of Chicago and had been very influential in Latin America, gave one example. He cited the example of a Chilean company that had paid US$150 million *in dollar bills* to buy an Argentine electrical company when a similar tax was adopted in Argentina. It took several days to count the money! He also reported that Argentine companies were paying their debts through Uruguayan accounts to avoid the Argentine tax on financial transactions. In time, barter would also replace some financial transactions. Some reporters interviewed me, and I spoke somewhat critically about the tax on checks. Then on September 7, 1993, the *Folha de São Paulo* ran an article, accompanied by a big picture of me, citing my comment that the tax on checks should be abolished.

At this time the Imposto Unico still had a large following. A paper by Augusto Jefferson Lemus reported on a survey of Congressmen conducted by Goes de Piquet Consultores Associados that found that fifty-eight percent of them favored this tax. The government had sold them on the idea that the revenue from this tax would be directed straight into investments in the rundown public health system. That system was the only door open to the poorest seventy percent of the population when they became ill. However, the government used these funds to service the public debt, to pay civil employees wages, pay pensions, and do basically everything but spend for healthcare for the poor. Still, the tax remained. Finally in 2007, the government announced that the tax would expire in 2008. I concluded that dreams and illusions never die. There was also a lot of discussion at the Symposium about the Brazilian VAT, a tax largely collected by the states. In Brazil the VAT raises a lot of money, almost more than in any other place in the world, but it is very distorting. Would a clearinghouse among the states, to apportion tax revenue, be possible? How would it work? These questions had been raised before and were raised again at the Symposium.

Harberger commented that he was surprised by the lack of concern or urgency among Brazilian policymakers and economists regarding the problem of inflation. As he put it: "With thirty-three percent inflation per month, what other index does one need to panic?" He speculated that before indexing was introduced, a little inflation created major social upheaval and forced governments to take corrective measures. But as indexing became more sophisticated, nations were more willing to cope with higher rates of inflation. Returning to Friedman's words, inflation was less painful with indexing. However, this was more likely to be true for the wealthier classes who were able to take actions to protect themselves. It was less true for the poorer classes, who were forced to hold their limited assets in cash. These assets lost value by the day. Thus, inflation was likely to have perverse effects on income distribution. Indexing had also been applied to government spending and to tax revenue. This had reduced the impact of inflation on tax revenue as expected from the Tanzi effect. That effect, based on one of my economic theories, predicted that when inflation becomes very high the value of the taxes that the government gets falls. The higher is the inflation rate, the greater is the revenue fall.

The lack of motivation to combat inflation reflected the lack of "voice" on the part of the poor. The higher classes had the mechanisms to cope with, and perhaps even profit from, inflation. Lending overnight operations on super short-term debt yielded two or even three percent daily (or nightly). Thus, inflation was not an equal problem for everyone. It was in part transferring wealth to the higher classes, while the poor suffered losses. This would explain why the plan that finally stopped inflation a couple years later became very popular with a large part of the population. Given the rate of inflation, the purchasing power of wages decreased by as much as one-third from the beginning to the end of the month. As a result, inflation increased income concentration in Brazil. When price stability finally came, the poor no longer suffered these losses.

Professor James Buchanan, the godfather of the public choice branch of economics and a Nobel Prize winner in economics in 1986, commented that during his visit to Brazil he had learned that the computer revolution, which in Brazil had spread quickly and deeply, had reduced popular resistance to inflation by making widespread indexing possible. Without computers, indexing would have been more rudimentary, less precise, and less attractive. Buchanan also addressed the economic role of constitutions, a topic of great interest to him. He stated that the appropriate use of a liberal constitution is not to lay down precise rules, as the Brazilian Constitution had done in 1988, but to restrict the economic role of the state. The state is the ultimate monopolist because of its power to impose taxes and punishments through the justice system; thus its power needs to be restricted and only a good constitution can do that. For Buchanan, the Swiss Constitution came closest to an ideal one because it was the most restrictive on the actions and economic power of the government.

The Constitution enacted on October 5, 1988 was the seventh in less than two hundred years of Brazilian independence, and the sixth in little over one hundred years of Brazil's history as a Republic. Prior constitutions were written in 1824, 1891, 1924, 1937, 1946, and 1967. Despite having numerous constitutions in such a short period of time, legislators were still eager to alter these documents. Major periodic revisions occurred to each of these constitutions. The constitution in force in 2009 is twenty one years old. However, by June 2006, it already had fifty-two amendments. Obviously, the Brazilian legal structure is very different from the Swiss paradigm advocated by Professor Buchanan. Contrary to the Swiss constitution, it is uniquely verbose and extends to over two hundred and fifty articles. In its original version, it assured special privileges and monopolies to state companies. The document limited or sometimes even prohibited foreign investment and competition and imposed restrictions on foreigners' rights to hold equity in Brazil. It also assured to Brazilians universal and absolute right to healthcare, a right that the poor public finances has made it difficult to satisfy at a satisfactory level of quality.

By the time of the symposium, there had been at least two hundred and twenty changes in the constitutions of Latin American countries. For example, Venezuela had changed its constitution every seven years since it had been enacted. Thus, what does it mean to rely on the constitution if it can be changed so easily? Several people at the Symposium questioned Buchanan's view. Was that view driven too much by the situation in the US, where it is very difficult to change the constitution? Buchanan replied that the exercise of drafting a constitution is itself important in order to teach people the importance of the rule of law. I had the impression that many at the conference did not agree with him.

Buchanan also sharply criticized President Clinton's reversal of the 1986 US tax reform. That reform was predicated on the view that the government should reduce its interference in the actions of individuals and enterprises, thus accepting their outcome. The 1986 U.S. tax reform had effectively introduced restrictions on the economic role of the state and especially on its role in creating "tax expenditures." Through these "tax expenditures" the government attempts to redirect individual spending towards particular categories that the government deems desirable, such as housing, charitable contributions, and health expenditures. Of course, the higher the tax rates, the more valuable the "tax expenditures" become for those who use them. Buchanan implied that the government had no right to do this because it changed the choices of taxpayers. The Clinton period would be characterized by a sharp increase in the use of these "tax expenditures." They would replace increases in public spending because the latter was constrained by a Republican Congress that at the time had no intention to let public spending go up. Ironically, the second Bush administration would return to the use of tax expenditures and public spending, thus distancing itself from pure conservative principles. Both Clinton and Bush would abandon the philosophy and the spirit that had guided the 1986 Reagan reform.

Buchanan's mention of the rule of law and its implication for economic relations and contracts reminded me of a charming painting I had seen in London at the National Gallery. The painting deserves to be published as an article in the *American Economic Review* and the painter to get a Nobel Prize in economics because he anticipated the concepts of "public good" and of "rule of law" by about five hundred years. These two concepts play an important role in modern economic thinking. Stefano di Giovanni, or Sassetta, was an early Renaissance Italian painter born in 1392. Between 1439 and 1444, he painted a seven- panel altarpiece on the life of St. Francis. One of the panels in the altarpiece illustrates the role that St. Francis played in an agreement between the inhabitants of Gubbio, a small, beautiful, medieval town in Central Italy, and a wolf that had been preying on the townspeople. According to the legend, St. Francis convinced the municipality to use public money to feed the wolf. He also convinced the wolf to stop preying on the people of Gubbio. Thus a "public good" (greater safety for all) would be financed with public money. The painting shows the wolf placing its right paw in the hand of St. Francis in the presence of a notary public who duly registers the contract. Citizens of Gubbio are shown watching the scene outside the city walls. The remains of people recently eaten by the wolf are clearly visible on the ground nearby, still dripping with blood. The wolf promises to abide by the "rule of law" that is by the agreement. As most modern public finance economists, Buchanan would probably approve of this use of public money for financing a genuine public good and the setting of a kind of constitutional mandate.

Returning to the symposium, one section of the conference dealt with social security reform in Brazil. In a speech by Antonio Brito, the Brazilian Minister of Social Security at that time, he defined the Brazilian social security system as a time bomb. However, it was a time bomb that would explode in the future, while politicians only seemed to worry about the present. The political cost-benefit evaluation of policies of this kind makes it unattractive to most politicians to deal with them. Why should they invest their present political capital to deal with a future problem? This is one reason why pension problems are so difficult to solve. It also suggests that, in some areas, rigorous ex ante evaluation of the costs and benefits (present and future) of policies should be required *before* a new policy is enacted. In some policy areas, as pensions, once mistakes are made they are difficult to correct.

The real problem with the pension system in Brazil is the unsustainable benefits system. Assured by prior legislation and upheld by the 1988 Constitution, the Supreme Court considers the benefits valid. Not only are public salaries very high, but they can also be many times higher than those in the private sector for the same functions. Besides, public servants are hardly ever fired and can retire after only thirty-five years of work with one hundred percent of active employees' wage. After a military serviceman dies, the government extends full lifelong pension to his widow and even to unmarried daughters. This may provide an incentive for them not to marry. Finally, all rural workers over sixty years of age are entitled to a minimum pension, regardless of any prior contribution.

There was some discussion of the Chilean model of privatizing part of the pension system, but the conclusion at the conference was that, in the Brazilian case, this would simply shift the problem to the budget. This is because the government would continue to pay pensions to those who retire or who have retired but would lose the contributions of younger workers. These younger workers, who would not be retiring for many years would be able to divert their contributions (their social security taxes) to private pension funds after the reform had been passed. This would increase the fiscal deficit. At the end of this session someone quoted three sentences from a speech by one of the generals during the military regime. The three sentences were:

> "We are facing an abyss."
> "Nobody will stop us."
> "We shall take a long step forward."

After the meeting, the group visited the Faculty of Law at the University of São Paulo. In this formal visit, during which the Brazilian National Anthem was played, we heard speeches by Professor Arnold Harberger, Delfim Netto, and Paulo Maluf, then the mayor of Sao Paulo. Together with Maluf and Delfim Netto, I gave a television interview on the tax on checks. I had the impression that the interviewers were using me to criticize the government. In these meetings, which were often half technical and half political, there was always the danger of not knowing the undercurrents and the political positions of the participants. However, I always tried to state my positions as honestly and as precisely as I could. Inevitably my statements were reported in the press and often they were amplified and attributed to the IMF rather than to my personal views. At that time, the high rate of inflation and its impact on taxes had given the "Tanzi effect" a great deal of notoriety. As an example, an editorial in the *Jornal do Brasil* of July 3, 1993 titled "Crepúsculo do Pajés," or "The Tribal Healers' Dawn," reported: "... economists are dominating public life and enjoy a high social prestige when they talk of Gini index and Tanzi effect..." I am afraid that the prestige of economists has fallen dramatically in more recent years and especially after the current crisis that they were unable to prevent or even to anticipate.

Maluf was a presidential candidate at the time. He was of Lebanese background and spoke several foreign languages. He was typical of the influence of the Lebanese, the heirs of the Phoenicians, in the world. They have been very successful emigrants who have done well economically and even politically in many countries. I was impressed in my travels by how often I found them, at times in places where little else was successful. They have shown a remarkable ability to adjust to local situations and to take advantage of any economic opportunities available to them. They must have in their genes the attitude for trade but also for successful professional and political lives. It is a pity that they have not succeeded in creating a stable Lebanon. I had a somewhat amusing illustration of the role of Lebanese immigrants when I visited the exhibition of Latin American paintings that would be sold at the 2008 annual Sotheby's auction in New York. A painting by Florencio Molina Campos (1891-1959) titled "La Fiesta" showed a street scene of people dancing in a typical Latin American small town while a band plays near a shop. The sign on the shop was "Almacen El Libano."

After the 1993 conference, I did not go back to Brazil until late 1995 but continued to track its developments. By this time Brazil had experimented with a so-called Heterodox Stabilization Plan that tied the Brazilian currency to a basket of strong international currencies. Though it was somewhat similar to the Convertibility Law introduced in Argentina in 1991, it did not attach the Brazilian currency solely to the dollar, as the Argentine law had done. In the process, it had succeeded in sharply reducing the inflation rate. There are two episodes from this period that may be worth reporting because of their implicit lessons. The first concerns Osiris Lopes Filho, the second Rubens Ricupero.

Osiris Lopes Filho was the director of taxation and customs in 1994. He was an attorney and a university professor with the reputation of being fully honest and very tough. In 1994, the Brazilian national soccer team won that most important sport event in the world that is the World Cup, played that year in the US. It is estimated that more people around the globe watch the final game of the World Cup than any other event on television. The winning country achieves great glory and fame, not to mention the economic benefits for the players. For example, Pele, the Brazilian soccer superstar, was knighted in 1997 by the Queen of England. When the French Team defeated Brazil and won the World Cup in 1998, President Chirac gave each player the Medal of Honor. Zinedine Zidane, who had guided the French team to victory by scoring two goals, became a very rich and famous man. The winning players become national heroes in the same way as victorious generals used to be in the past. This is especially true in Latin America where soccer is not just a sport but a religion. For example, in May 2006, there were major prison riots in São Paulo that caused more than a hundred deaths. One of the rioters' main demands was guaranteed access to televisions during the forthcoming World Cup in Germany, the one which the French would ultimately win.

In 1994, when the Brazilian World Cup champions returned home from their "heroic" enterprise, they arrived at the airport with seventeen tons of merchandise that they had acquired during their tour of American cities. As the law required, this merchandise had to be inspected at customs and taxed accordingly. Therefore, the players were asked to open their bags and to pay customs. Lopes Filho was a firm believer in the rule of law and maintained that all are equal before the law, even World Cup champions. The problem was that thousands of fans were waiting outside the airport to welcome home the heroes. Opening all the bags and inspecting seventeen tons of merchandise took hours. This delayed the beginning of the welcoming parade and made the fans and the players very angry. Many felt that the situation justified the suspension of the rule of law. Not only that, but several players and team managers also felt entitled to tax-free imports. After all, they were the World Cup champions, and this should come with some privileges. This idea might sound outrageous, but the Brazilian public largely supported it. Osiris Lopes Filho stood his ground and in the process became a *former* head of taxation. Rubens Ricupero, then the Economic Minister, fired him for having done his job of enforcing the rule of law. Ultimately, Lopes Filho had made his point that the conscience of a tax evader is black, even if the evader is a World Cup hero. Lopes Filho was also the man who had estimated that over six hundred Brazilians with incomes in the millions of U.S. dollars paid little or nothing in taxes. I am sure that these people were happy to see him go.

Lopes Filho was not the first customs director to be fired for enforcing the rule of law. I met another one in Tunisia in the early 1980s. He had been fired when he tried to tax the car that Tunisian President Bourghiba's daughter was bringing back to Tunisia after completing her studies in France. The director insisted that the law was equal for all, even for the daughter of the President, and because of that he also became a *former* director.

Maybe it was poetic justice or simply coincidence that a short time later, Rubens Ricupero, the Minister of Economy who had fired Lopes Filho, was forced to resign. Ricupero had been a distinguished diplomat typical of the high quality produced by Itamaraty, the Brazilian school for diplomats. He spoke several languages, was a very cultured person, and, before becoming Minister of Economy, had been the Brazilian ambassador to Washington. He had been a leading candidate for President of the World Trade Organization, but Renato Ruggiero, an Italian diplomat, would become the head of the WTO instead.

Ricupero's difficulties came when, during a private conversation with a reporter after a press conference, he mistakenly believed that the microphones had been switched off and admitted that the government was manipulating the inflation indices. As he put it: "I don't have any scruples; what is good, we use, what is bad, we hide." Because the satellite transmission was still on, this statement was recorded and broadcast at prime time national news.

It will be recalled that inflation indices were used to index wages, and wages were used to index pensions. Thus these indices were very important for many individuals, such as wage earners and pensioners, but they were also important for the public finances. As is well known, the measurement of inflation is not an easy matter, and it is possible that these indices overstate the rates for some groups while understating it for others. Minister Ricupero had simply tried to lighten the burden on the public finances, which were very much in the red. He was forced to resign and was sent as the Ambassador of Brazil at the splendid Brazilian embassy in Piazza Navona in Rome from which he could admire the famous Bernini statues and fountains. Thus, he was hardly in exile, especially since his ancestors had come from Puglia (the region of Italy where I was born!). He later became the head of UNCTAD, a UN agency.

The Heterodox Stabilization Plan, the one that finally broke the inflation spiral, was very popular, especially among the poorer classes, who were not as well equipped as the wealthy to protect themselves against high inflation. These poorer people had suffered the erosion of their cash assets due to the high rate of inflation and thus welcomed the price stability and the increase in real income that came with the plan. However, government finances benefited much less from the fall in prices because almost everything had been indexed (both public spending and tax liabilities toward the government). Thus, despite the predictions of the "Tanzi effect" and contrary to the example of Argentina after the convertibility plan of the early 1990s, the stabilization in prices did not generate significant extra revenue for the Brazilian government. In reality, Brazilian public finances remained in a precarious condition.

CHAPTER 4

BRAZIL: FROM INFLATION BACK TO GROWTH

In December of 1996, I went back to Brazil for a conference in Salvador de Bahia, the beautiful city in Northeast Brazil. The IMF, in collaboration with the finance secretaries of the Brazilian states and the representatives of the Brazilian Ministry of Finance, organized the conference. Salvador was one of the earliest cities built by the Portuguese in Brazil in the middle of the sixteenth century and was the capital of Brazil until 1763, when the capital was moved to Rio. It is now the capital of the state of Bahia. It faces a huge harbor on All Saints' Bay.

The main issue of the conference was the perennial one of reforming Brazil's two VATs: one imposed by the states, and a less important one, on industrial products, imposed by the national government. The first of these taxes creates major economic distortions but generates a lot of revenue. In terms of revenue it is one of the most productive value added taxes in the world. The challenge has been how to reform it without losing revenue. This had been one of the major objectives of the tax mission that I had led in 1992 but, as reported earlier, nothing came out of that mission. The difficulty of reforming tax systems under these circumstances strengthened my belief that fiscal federalism, a policy whereby sub-national governments acquire a lot of political and economic power, can become a major obstacle to tax reform because it reduces the freedom of national policymakers, among other problems. I have seen this problem in several countries including Argentina and India. Thus, countries contemplating the introduction of fiscal decentralization, accompanied by delegation of political power to sub-national governments, should take into account the important and likely future cost that may accompany this policy. In Brazil it has been impossible up to now (August 2009) to agree on a reform acceptable to all the states and to the national government. In March 2008 the Brazilian federal government again advanced proposals aimed at reforming the VAT. It remains to be seen how successful it will be this time.

The first night of the conference we attended a dinner at the famous fish restaurant, Bergaça. On the following Sunday, Bahia state's finance secretary, Rodolpho Tourinho, invited us to visit Pelourinho, the old area of Salvador. Pelourinho was the original port of entry for African slaves who were then sold to landowners mostly to work in the fields. It had become a slum area over the years but, because of its historical importance and its potential tourist value, at the time of the conference it was being restored as an historical center. It is a very attractive area with beautiful plazas, old churches and picturesque streets. Pelourinho historic center became part of UNESCO World Heritage Sites about twenty years ago.

We visited the Church of São Francisco and the Cathedral. Both are splendid examples of baroque churches built in the New World during the seventeenth century, when Brazil was a Portuguese colony. Salvador was one of the first and grandest cities built in the New World. The Church of São Francisco, referred to as "the gold church," offers an extreme and splendid example of baroque architecture. It is estimated that it was decorated with three tons of gold. One interesting characteristic of this church is the marvelous woodcarvings that represent naked and obviously pregnant women. These women are holding the columns in the Church. Pregnancy must have been related to sin because of its association with sexual activities. To become pregnant the women must have had intercourse, which implied that they had sinned. Therefore, they had to spend a period of penitence after giving birth. Holding the columns in the church for eternity must have been the penitence. I presume that there was no penitence for the men because there was no reference to them in the church.

Right next to São Francisco we visited a third-order Franciscan church with an incredibly ornate façade. At some point in the past, and for unknown reasons, the front of the church was covered with white stucco, which concealed the ornaments. It was not until the 1930s, when an electrician was doing work on the building, that the ornaments were rediscovered. After the Franciscan church, we visited the nearby Cathedral of Salvador de Bahia. This is another breathtaking church, but unfortunately some of its wonderful woodcarvings have been badly damaged by termites. It is located right next to the oldest medical school in South America, which actually began as a school for barbers, and then progressed into a school for midwives.

Pelourinho is a very picturesque area, reminiscent of the medieval, historical centers of old European cities. As mentioned, it had been a slum area for decades when Salvador was a very poor city with high unemployment. The people living there, many of whom had been abusively occupying buildings after the legal owners moved away, were given some financial incentives to vacate the apartments or houses in which they had been living. Now the area has lots of typical restaurants, coffee shops, art shops, and other interesting places.

In the whole city of Salvador de Bahia, but especially in Pelourinho, one notices a strong African influence, with eighty percent of the population being of African descent. The African influence is especially evident from the mixing of African gods with Christian divinities. As Roger Bastide, a student of the matter wrote: "Catholicism superimposed itself on the African religion rather than replacing it." Thus, it became almost like the stucco on the front of the third-order Franciscan Church. When you remove the façade, you find the original African religions. In Felipe Fernandez-Armesto's *The Americas: A Hemispheric History*, he cites Nina Rodriguez, a sociologist of religion, who comments that Africans simply borrowed the camouflage from Christianity, not the doctrine. For the Africans, their core religious beliefs did not change, only the external expression of it did change. In a shop that we visited, there were donations of cigarettes, money, and even beer to an African god. Thus, the African god was not immune to common sins. The African influence is also evident in the popularity of voodoo, locally called *Macumba*. Tourists could even witness voodoo shows, but unfortunately lack of time prevented us from seeing one. However, one wonders how authentic these shows organized for tourists really are.

In Pelourinho there was a lot of naïf art. The similarity to the naïf paintings of Haiti was striking. The colors were the same and even some of the imaginary scenes. This implied that the inhabitants of Salvador de Bahia had come from the same regions in Africa as those in Haiti. As in Haiti, there was a lot of repetition in the artwork. Once a talented artist comes forward with a new style, less talented painters often copy that style. In a way, this is the inevitable commercialization of art. This commercialization of art made me think of economic theory where innovative papers by top economists are often followed by their epigones, who introduce but small variations to the original works. The new papers occupy journals' space but contribute little to our understanding of how economies work.

One evening the governor invited us to his house for dinner, and I suggested to him that he should sponsor a good book on Bahia's naïf painters. These painters remain unknown outside of Bahia. They could become as profitable an export for the state as they have been for Haiti. I bought four paintings, one considerably more expensive than the others by a painter called Calixto Sales, who I was told had acquired some fame. The other three were nice and cheap because the painters were still unknown. In 2005, following a tradition initiated a few years earlier, my family and I used one of these cheaper paintings to make Christmas cards.

Salvador de Bahia is indeed a beautiful city that is making a great effort to attract tourism. It will be even nicer when all the work on Pelourinho is completed and when the restructuring of the beach area along the sea is finished. There is however some concern that the development may damage the historical authenticity of Salvador. Visiting this city as well as other baroque cities of Brazil and other Latin American countries one often has the impression of being in Southern Europe. This impression is derived from the architecture, especially that of the churches. The areas that had been colonized by the Spaniards or the Portuguese have extraordinarily beautiful churches. This development did not touch North America, with the exception of Mexico where cities such as Mexico City and Puebla give the same impression. In Puebla, the Iglesia de Santo Domingo de

Guzman built in 1571 is an incredible church that could compete with many churches in Rome. The Cathedral in the Zócalo, the main plaza in Mexico City, is also an extraordinary one. Perhaps because of the religious background of the early immigrants to the new continent, or because of the poverty of the land where the early immigrants settled at the time, the United States lost out in terms of historical building, especially beautiful baroque churches. This is probably due to the fact that most early immigrants to the US came from countries that had experienced the cultural changes of the Reformation in Europe. Richly decorated churches were not part of the cultural environment from which these immigrants came.

Later that evening, back in the hotel, I turned on the television and heard the sad news of three Italian tourists who had arrived that morning and had gone swimming. All three had drowned, pulled by strong currents. Immediately following this story, an infomercial came on. In the advertisement, two men, a Brazilian and an American, claimed that they could make tumors disappear by "graça de Deus," or burned by the "grace of God." They gave the number of a checking account where one could send the advance payment for this service. They claimed that they could cure anything, including AIDS, for a price, of course. The American was appropriately named Tommy O'Cell, and the Brazilian evangelical minister R.R. Soares. It seemed as if these two men could sell ice to the Eskimos. I have always been amazed by the ability of men like these to sell their services. However, it also made me less surprised at the ability of politicians to sell miracle cures for economic ills.

During the conference, we observed the finance secretaries of the Brazilian states in action as they tweaked the Brazilian tax system, thus making it more complex. A particular state would propose a tax incentive or a tax modification for a specific activity. For example, it would propose to exempt taxi cars from the value added tax. An incentive requested by a state would have to be approved by the National Fiscal Policy Council (CONFAZ in Portuguese) that included the finance secretaries from all the states, before it could be accepted. But once CONFAZ approved the incentive for the state that had proposed it, all the other states could and were likely to adopt it. It was unlikely that proposals would be made, or accepted, aimed at the elimination of an incentive. I thought that I was observing a case of "fiscal termites" at work on the foundation of the Brazilian tax system because this was a cumulative process that could gradually bring about major changes as the real termites had done with the wood carvings of the cathedral.

I heard that at one of these meetings a proposal had been approved to reduce the rate of the VAT for the front part of a cow. The argument behind this proposal was that the meat from that part of the cow is less desirable and is thus bought by the poor. The assumption was that this change would help the poor. However, the result was that soon most cows had just the front! The meat from the rear of the cow disappeared from the market. After this meeting I used the terminology of "fiscal termites" in some of my writing to describe the impact that globalization and technological developments were having on tax systems. The point that I wanted to make was that in slow and subtle ways globalization was damaging the foundations of tax systems. This would make it more difficult for countries to maintain high levels of taxation.

In July 1998, I went back to Brasília to participate in a conference on "Income Distribution, Poverty and Growth." The Ministry of Agricultural Development and the World Bank organized the conference, with Raul Jungmann, then the Minister of Agricultural Development, as chair. Professor Joseph Stiglitz, then the Chief Economist at the World Bank, represented the bank and contributed a paper on "Distribution, Efficiency and Voice."

The Conference resulted in a Brazilian book, entitled *Distribuição de Riqueza e Crescimento Econômico*, and in a "Declaration of Brasília" that contained ten important points related to income distribution. These points stressed the responsibility of the government vis-à-vis improving opportunities for the poorest groups and the importance of land distribution in the case of Brazil. Economists connected with the "structuralist school", of which Celso Furtado had been a leading exponent, had stressed the importance of land reform back in the 1950s and 1960s but in more recent years this policy had lost some of its attraction. I contributed a chapter to the book in which I stressed fundamental determinants of income distribution, including social norms and what the state could do about them. I argued that these norms had received little or no attention on the part of economists but that they could prove to be important. For example, if rich people marry only rich people, the income distribution is less likely to improve.

I went back to Brasília in September 1998 to attend an International Seminar on Public Finance. Brasília still looked like a planned city in search of an identity. I still had the feeling that the buildings had been placed in the middle of nowhere even though I once again marveled at the architectural beauty and especially at the stunningly beautiful Ministry of Foreign Affairs (Palacio Itamaraty) which seems to be a mirage coming out of water. The seminar commemorated the creation of the highly computerized and centralized Brazilian Treasury system. Through the technical assistance of the IMF, which had employed some Brazilian experts, features of this system had made their way into countries such as Russia and Hungary. This is the mysterious way in which knowledge or particular practices sometimes spread.

The seminar opened on September 2 at the National School of Public Administration (ENAP). This school, located some distance from the city, is housed in an immense complex, the construction of which had been financed by the German government some years earlier. The opening of the conference was a formal and grand occasion. The then president of Brazil, Henrique Cardoso, and a former president, José Sarney, attended. I was placed at the table with them and with the Minister of Finance, Pedro Malan, and the Director of the Treasury, Murilo Portugal. Before the opening ceremony, I met privately with President Cardoso, who was gracious enough to say that he remembered me from earlier encounters when he was Minister of Finance and had visited my office at the IMF in Washington.

After the President's and the Minister's opening speeches, I gave my talk. It was a somewhat blunt statement that warned that a fiscal adjustment would be necessary to prevent a debt explosion. This was a difficult period for Brazil because foreign financing had become very expensive. Southeast Asia was in the middle of a financial crisis and Russia had just undergone debt default. Brazil was running high fiscal deficits, its public debt was rising, and it had to be financed at very high rates. The real interest rate on government debt had reached twelve percent, discouraging private investment and contributing to the increase in the ratio of debt to GDP. Most of the debt was external and it was several times the annual exports. In 1998 the Brazilian situation looked much more precarious than that of Argentina. In my talk I outlined some of the necessary adjustments, stressing the need to reduce public spending that was already very high and growing fast. There were about seven hundred people attending the conference including reporters from major newspapers and television stations.

Following my talk, Pedro Malan stated that he agreed with my assessment. I should add that by this time the problem of inflation had largely disappeared, thanks to the Stabilization Plan; however, the fiscal problem remained, and this was becoming increasingly a balance of payment problem because of the large external component of the public debt. The government in power at this time was a very good one from a technical point of view and was fully aware of need to deal with this challenge. It had inherited the problem and had to find solutions that could be implemented. The constitutional reform of 1988 had reduced executive power and freedom so that the government was unable to implement some of the policy changes that were necessary to correct the existing imbalances. For this reason my statement did not annoy Minister Malan, as would have normally been the case. On the contrary he saw it as an endorsement of what he wanted to do.

I had to answer various questions in a press conference following Malan's statement. The next day the major newspapers reported my talk in front page articles. *O Estado de São Paulo* reported that for the IMF the increase in public debt was not sustainable and that the "Real," the new Brazilian currency, was at risk. *Folha de São Paulo* focused on my criticism of what the government had done, and especially not done, in the previous year in the fiscal area. Other newspapers reported my criticism of the growth in unproductive public spending and especially pensions and the salaries of public employees. I was embarrassed by the fact that my statement had attracted more attention than the statements of the President and the Minister. To add insult to injury, in *O Globo*, the caption for a large picture of the conference panel read: "Mr. Tanzi and the President of Brazil, the President of the Senate, and the Minister." On the following day, a major morning television program invited me as a guest. I was tired but fairly relaxed and answered the questions, which were posed to me in Portuguese, in Spanish mixed with some Portuguese words. The program's host seemed pleased by my answers, though I had my own strong doubts about my performance.

A few months later I went back to Brasília and to the National School of Public Administration to attend a conference jointly sponsored by ENAP and by the OECD Development Center in Paris. At the time the head of the OECD Development Center was a Frenchman, appropriately named Jean Bonvin (John Good Wine). They had organized a luncheon for the speakers at an Italian restaurant called Partenopeo. Place cards had been set on the table and Bonvin's name had been misspelled as Mr. Bovin (Mr. Cow). He seemed amused but confessed that he preferred to be Mr. Bonvin.

I had been asked to give a paper on the changes that had occurred on the economic role of the state over recent decades in developing countries. I enjoyed writing this paper because it related nicely to some work that I had been doing with Ludger Schuknecht, a German economist. Two years later, that work would result in a book, *The Growth of Public Spending in the Twentieth Century*, published by Cambridge University Press. In my paper I showed how thinking about what the state should or should not do in the economic sphere had changed especially in the two most recent decades. This was the time after the so-called Washington Consensus had given more prominence to the role of private markets but during the crisis of Southeast Asian countries of 1997-98, when doubts were being raised about whether markets were as efficient as claimed.

The Washington Consensus stressed the important role of *policies* without giving enough attention to the role of *institutions*. To some extent, institutions are the instruments that deliver the policies and that ensure that the policies are not distorted during their implementation. This distortion can happen when the individuals who manage the institutions have incentives that conflict with the goals of the government and these individuals have the power to act on their incentives. In these situations what economists call "principal-agents problems" can become serious. The Washington Consensus reflected a rather optimistic view of the role of markets and of policies and advocated a limited role of the state even in regulating the market. The paper was well received by the participants in the conference and by *Gazeta Mercantil*, a Brazilian business newspaper specializing in economic issues. It ran a long article summarizing the paper and quoting me to the effect that market economies might not survive if governments do not pay intelligent attention to the problem of uneven income distribution. This is a concern that I continue to have to this day.

The period immediately after 1998 was not a good one for Brazil. The problem that I had highlighted in my talk at the 1998 conference unfortunately got worse in spite of the government's efforts to contain it. The government was politically unable to contain the growth of public spending. To deal with the fiscal problem, the level of taxation increased substantially. However, largely because of earmarking and indexation, public spending kept going up even faster so that the fiscal deficit was not contained by the tax increase. The crisis in Southeast Asia spilled over into Brazil creating an urgent need for a large program of financial assistance on the part of the IMF. For a while there was the fear that Brazil would experience the same difficulties as the countries of Southeast Asia and Russia. The consequence of the South Asian Crisis of 1998 was the overnight devaluation of the Brazilian Real from R$1.20 to R$1.80 to the dollar in early January 1999. The currency maintained this downward trend, and in October 2002 reached R$ 4.00 to the dollar. This made Brazilian exports very competitive. In recent years the Real appreciated as a consequence of reasonable policies and the commodity boom that was very beneficial to Brazil. By mid 2008 the Real had appreciated to about R$1.70 to the US$.

Brazil's currency devaluation had a negative impact on its southernmost neighbor. Argentina was suffering from its monetary rule that kept its exchange rate at parity with the US dollar, while Brazil bent its exchange rates on the aftermath of the Asian, Russian, and Turkish crisis. The devaluation in 1999 sharply reduced export prices for Brazilian products. Throughout 2000 and 2001, these prices were further reduced. Benefiting from MERCOSUR, a South American common market started in 1994, Brazil increasingly exported goods to member countries and to the rest of the world. The country also attracted some auto and other manufacturing companies. While good for Brazil, its policies in this period made the problems of Argentina worse. Argentina defaulted on its debt and experienced its deepest recession in 2002, when its GDP fell by 10.9 percent. While Brazil was not the major factor, its role in the Argentine debacle was clearly significant. I described the Argentine experience in my 2007 book, *Argentina: an Economic Chronicle.*

As there are perfect storms, there can also be perfect weathers. Brazil experienced these good weathers in recent years when many things seemed to align themselves in such a way to bring major benefits to the country. In recent years the Brazilian economy benefited from high commodity prices and from a large international demand for some of its industrial products, such as cars, cell phones, steel and planes. China's and India's rapid growth has also been advantageous for Brazil because of the high demand for Brazilian products. As a result of this good export performance, Brazil has been able to repay the loans obtained from the IMF. It has had large annual trade surpluses, and has accumulated large foreign exchange. It has made significant institutional reforms that have helped control the economic problems that the country had been facing in earlier years. However, taxation has reached the level of around thirty-eight percent of GDP, which is considered very high for a developing country. It will need to drastically change its tax system, and reduce its weight on the economy. To do so it is faced with the difficult task of reducing public spending.

Crime remains a problem and the attempt to improve the distribution of income has been only partly successful. Income distribution in Brazil, one of the most uneven in the world, has improved during the Lula government partly because of large transfers to the poor. But programs like Bolsa Familia, a highly praised program that transfers resources to poor families, may not be financially sustainable in the long run and may not bring durable changes to the income distribution. On the positive side inflation has remained low. The change in government from Cardoso to Lula did not bring the major economic shock that some had feared. The orthodox policies of Central Bank chairman and former Bank of Boston Global CEO Henrique Meirelles have successfully reduced public debt exposure to foreign exchange risk and to short term volatility. These policies have also reduced interest rates to a more sustainable level. This may have been President Lula's most outstanding achievement. Nevertheless, high and complex taxes combined with still high real interest rates and too many regulations continue to be major long-term obstacles to the growth of the economy. For the period through 2008, the commodity boom has been a great help to Brazil and has compensated for those obstacles.

In 2005, I went back to Brazil to speak at a conference on tax competition in Brasília. I do not have specific impressions from this short visit except taking several splendid photos of some of the major architectural highlights of the city, such as the Ministry of Foreign Affairs, the Brazilian Congress, and the Cathedral. I tried to document Brasilia's growth from a planned city into a real city with character. These photos were included in a photo exhibition that I had in Italy in September 2007. In March 2008, I returned to Rio to speak at a conference organized by the Instituto Brazileiro de Etica Concurrencial (ETCO). At the conference, I had been asked to speak on the "causes and consequences of the underground economy." In the late 1970s, when "underground economy" started attracting attention, I had been among the first economists to write papers on this phenomenon. In 1979 I had written a paper, issued as a working paper of the IMF and published in 1980 in an economic journal, in which I developed an econometric method—later commonly referred to as the "currency demand approach"—that could be used to get estimates of the size of the underground economy. The currency demand approach was based on the assumption that transactions in the underground economy are often conducted in cash so that a growing underground economy will lead to a growing demand for cash. If the additional demand for cash could be estimated using econometric techniques, making assumptions on the velocity of circulation of that cash, one could get an estimate of the size of the underground economy.

My method had been developed for, and applied to, the underground economy in the United States. One of its key assumptions was that higher income taxes lead to larger underground activities as individuals try to avoid paying these taxes. Thus, the underground activities would increase the demand for cash. The use of cash would replace that of checks that leave traces. Other variables were shown to influence the demand for cash so that they had to be taken into account in the econometric estimations. Soon, however, other economists began applying the method, at times with minor modifications, to estimate the underground economy of other countries. It became a widely used method for estimating the underground economy.

Over time I grew concerned about this development, given the rising confusion that accompanied the concept of underground economy. Some confused it with the informal economy. Some thought that it was identical to tax evasion. Some understood it as the national income not measured by the statistical offices. Soon there was "measurement without theory" and then great confusion about what precisely was being measured—was it tax evasion, income not accounted for by the national accounts authorities, informal activities or what? I also became uneasy about what I considered extravagant claims about the size of the underground economy and about its consequences made by some economists. Thus, after writing a few papers and publishing the first English language book on the subject in the early 1980s, I stopped writing on it. However, I continued to follow the topic, in part through papers that economic journals sent me to referee.

In 1999, at the invitation of the *Economic Journal*, the official journal of the British Royal Economic Society, I returned to the topic. In my paper, titled "Uses and Abuses of the Underground Economy," I criticized the application of inflated—and most likely incorrect—estimates of the underground economy. These estimates were being used to make all kinds of claims—that GDPs were greatly underestimated, that most of those classified as unemployed were busy working underground, that tax revenue could go up sharply if only the underground economy were taxed, and so on. The estimates were also used to stake particular political claims to certain groups, such as G-7, G-20, etc., which depended on the estimated size of a country's national income. Some claimed that Italy had become part of the G-7 group by inflating its GDP through a re-estimation of its underground economic activity.

At the ETCO conference in Rio de Janeiro, I was one of the two main speakers. The other was Professor Frederick Schneider, an economics professor from Austria, who greatly contributed to the literature on underground economy and especially to that aimed at measuring the phenomenon in many countries. ETCO, an association representing large enterprises, was interested in the phenomenon of underground economy because of the belief that: (a) the size of the underground economy had become very large in Brazil, and (b) due to the unfair competition, it was creating competitive difficulties for large enterprises that could not escape the burdens of taxes and rigid regulations. Producers working underground did not face these costs and thus could undersell the large enterprises. Some economists at ETCO had developed an index suggesting that the problem was a major one in Brazil, and Professor Schneider had estimated the size of the underground economy in Brazil in 2008 at over forty percent of GDP.

In my intervention, I outlined the causes (high taxes and excessive regulations) and the consequences (distorted statistics, unfair competition for law abiding enterprises) of a large underground economy. I questioned the significance of the estimate while stressing that the phenomenon still merited attention. I pointed out that an underground economy of more than forty percent of GDP, if considered additional to the official statistics of GDP, as it was interpreted, would imply that Brazil was more than forty percent richer than assumed from the official GDP. Therefore, Brazil's tax burden of about thirty-seven percent, when measured against the official size of the economy, would be reduced to about twenty-six percent if related to a GDP that was forty percent larger. This would raise questions about the common assumption shared by the International Finance Corporation (IFC) of the World Bank, by the World Economic Forum, and by many observers including those from ETCO that had placed Brazil among the countries of the world with the heaviest and most complex tax systems. This was clearly not a conclusion that the Instituto Brazileiro de Etica Concurrencial wanted. In my talk, I stressed that (a) the phenomenon of the underground economy was an important one because it affected the working of the market and the ethics of a competitive system, (b) that it should not be assumed that the national accounts authorities are underestimating GDP by such a large amount, and that (c) it should not be assumed that all those working underground would be part of the official labor force. Many of these workers are pensioners, minors, immigrants or simply people working a few hours at home or over the weekend.

The Conference, held at the Sofitel Hotel in Copacabana, was well organized and well attended. Several prominent Brazilians spoke about the problem of high and excessively complex taxation, about too many rigid regulations, especially in the labor market, and about how the above were affecting the economy. There were complaints about the stealing of electricity from electrical companies with unauthorized hookups and about the alleged unwillingness of the government to do anything about it. These statements were undermined in their impact by the release, the same morning of the conference, of the official statistics for the growth of the economy in 2007: the economy had grown at 5.4 percent, which was considered a very good rate. Clearly the commodity boom and relatively orthodox macroeconomic policies pursued by the Lula government were giving good results in a world situation that was very favorable to Brazilian exports. However, I felt that, given Brazil's potential and the very favorable international situation, without the constraints that it faced, Brazil should perhaps be growing at much higher rates, rates as high as those of China, India, and other countries.

CHAPTER 5

FOCUSING ON BAROQUE BRAZIL

The day after the ETCO conference in Rio, my wife and I flew to Belo Horizonte, the capital of Minas Gerais, drawn by the reputation of its famous baroque churches. In Belo Horizonte two members of the state police met us at the airport. They would accompany us during the three days of the visit. The escort had been provided by Paulo Páiva, whom I had met at the Inter-American Development Bank (IDB) in Washington when he was its vice president. He had also been the Brazilian Minister of Labor. He was now the president of the Development Bank of the State of Minas Gerais. He wanted to be sure that we had a safe and enjoyable visit in his region. One of the two escorts was a female lieutenant in the military police of Minas Gerais. She reminded us of the actress Sonia Braga from the film, *Doña Flor and Her Two Husbands*. She was lively, attractive, and spoke good English so that we much enjoyed her company. The other escort was a younger man, also a member of the police, who did not speak English and concentrated mostly on the driving.

After we checked into a hotel in Belo Horizonte we embarked on the itinerary that had been prepared beforehand in order to maximize what we would see during our three days in Minas Gerais. The name of the state means "general mines," and it comes from the fact that this is the area of Brazil rich in mineral resources including iron, precious stones, and at one time gold. Our first destination was Inhotim, a center of contemporary art. We had no idea what this place was and thought that "contemporary art" meant mainly paintings and sculptures by contemporary artists. We were thus surprised when the car left the city and, once out of the city, drove for more than an hour along winding, rural roads that were often not well kept. Over the years, because of other spending pressures, Brazil has spent little to upgrade its physical infrastructure. As we drove on, the area became progressively more rural, and we went through several villages before we finally arrived at Inhotim.

Having opened in 2005, Inhotim illustrates a new concept for an art museum. It is essentially a beautiful garden, truly an exotic paradise, with some works of art, mainly statues, distributed throughout the garden, a small lake in the middle, and some buildings containing indoor, contemporary art. The garden occupies 80 acres of land. The little lake has many swans both white and black. I had never seen black swans before and, after reading *The Black Swan: The Impact of the Highly Improbable* by Nassim Nicholas Taleb, I never would have thought that I would see one, let alone more than one in a given place. Taleb had used the black swan as a metaphor for highly improbable events referring mainly to the financial and stock market. But here there were several black swans, and the entire garden was truly a feast for our eyes. The artwork in the middle of the trees seemed indigenous to the landscape. The place had been a private plantation and was developed as a museum with the help of Roberto Burle Marx, a Brazilian *paisagista*. The original owner of Inhotim had been an American called Senhor Tim. The combination of Senhor and Tim had given the place the name of Inhotim.

The buildings contain avant-garde artwork, mainly by German artists. It is interesting work, but also the type of art that makes one wonder whether it is truly art or it is a joke being played on the viewer. A large, white and bare room contains many black "speakers" that, when they are turned on, produce the sound of Gregorian chants. Each speaker reproduces the chant of one monk. Another room is a kind of living room in which all is red. In another room, the floor is covered by broken glass on which visitors have to walk. In any case, despite the fact that it is far from the city center, the whole complex is definitely worth visiting. When we visited it, it was almost empty, but we were told that on weekends it is more crowded because people come from Belo Horizonte. Few come from further away. We hoped that it would have success and took many pictures that might be able to capture the beauty of this unique place.

In the evening, we returned to Belo Horizonte and had a lovely dinner with Mr. and Mrs. Páiva and with Mr. and Mrs. Ricardo Santiago at an Italian restaurant called Vecchio Sogno, or "old dream." Ricardo Santiago was the President of the Funducão João Pinheiro, a university-level school of public administration similar to the French ENA or to the national one in Brasília. It is a public school that trains functionaries for the government of Minas Gerais.

The existence of a state development bank and a state higher school of public administration gives a clear example of the power of the Brazilian states. Both of these institutions are financed by, and serve exclusively the objectives of, the state of Minas Gerais. Our escorts were also of the military police of Minas Gerais. As in the United States, in Brazil, fiscal decentralization (or fiscal federalism) is the result of historical developments. The power of the states, protected by the Constitution, has often created major macro-economic difficulties for the central government. In the 1990s, some of the states had amassed large public debts, some of which were owed to foreigners, forcing the national government to come to their rescue. A Fiscal Responsibility Law introduced in the late 1990s has reduced the degrees of freedom of the states. However, like in the United States, they continue to have a lot of power. As mentioned earlier it has been difficult to create an efficient tax system because the main tax base (the VAT) has remained a state tax and thus suffers from the differences created between the states. It should be added that in countries as large as Brazil and the US, it would be difficult to have a unitary (central) system of government that could control the whole territory. Minas Gerais alone is twice the size of Spain.

The morning following our dinner at the Italian restaurant, we planned to see a church designed by Oscar Neimeyer. However, it was raining hard so that we decided to go directly to our next major destination, Ouro Preto, about sixty miles from Belo Horizonte. When we arrived there, the mayor of Ouro Preto, Angelo Osualdo, received us at City Hall. Osualdo is a very cultured gentleman who speaks perfect English and French and who is the leading authority on Brazilian baroque. He was courteous and gave us a beautiful, illustrated book on Ouro Preto. He told us that since it was the day of Lent, in the evening there would be a procession with original Brazilian baroque music that we might find enjoyable and interesting.

After leaving the Prefectura we drove to the Pousada do Mondego, the hotel where we would be staying for the night. A *pousada* is a kind of guesthouse that functions as a small hotel. The Pousada do Mondego occupies a restored house of 1747 and is located very near the famous church of St. Francis of Assisi. The hotel is absolutely charming and contains original, antique furniture and objects that make it a genuine, little museum. It has also the advantage of being one block away from Praça Tiradentes (Tiradentes Plaza), the main square of the town. It overlooks a beautiful valley and in front of it there is an outdoor market where artisans sell their wares, mainly carvings made out of local stones. Some of the carvings are of very good artistic quality. Half of the carvings represent religious figures. The other half represents mostly beautiful, nude women.

Ouro Preto was founded in 1698 when gold was discovered on the bed of Rio Maranhão nearby. The subsequent gold rush was the biggest one in the Americas at that time, and the city grew so rapidly that the population soon reached one hundred fifty thousand. At that time the population of Ouro Preto was larger than that of any North American city. It is now only about eighty thousand people. Because the gold was mixed with iron it was black thus giving the city the name of Black Gold, or Ouro Preto, in Portuguese. Its wealth enabled the building of twenty-two beautiful churches and the first opera house in the Americas. It is an absolutely charming town that seems to be a reproduction in the real of one of those "ville imaginaire" that the naïf Haitian painter Prefet Duffaux has made popular. In some ways it seems unreal. Its streets are narrow, paved with cobblestones, and lined with multicolored houses. The whole thing looks truly like a naïf painting. Not surprisingly, it is one of the sites recognized by UNESCO as a World Heritage Site. The town climbs on steep hills with churches occupying the "commanding heights." The churches truly dominate the city. They are visible from any point. Built mostly during the gold rush of the eighteenth century, they are very ornate and their interior is often covered by gold leaves. They are not very large but are among the most beautiful baroque churches to be found anywhere. They are true jewels.

After leaving our luggage at the hotel we walked steeply uphill to Praça Tiradentes to begin our visit of Ouro Preto. Praça Tiradentes was named after the leader of an independence movement against the Portuguese, Inconfidencia Mineira. He was nicknamed Tiradentes because he was a barber-dentist then a particular occupation because barbers were those who pulled bad teeth. There were no dentists at that time. The Portuguese arrested him and executed him in Rio, prominently displaying his severed head to suppress the independence movement. Tiradentes is now recognized as a major historical figure in Brazil and monuments to him have been erected in Ouro Preto and Rio, among other places.

Our first stop was the Museum of Science and Techniques of the School of Minas Gerais, which houses the Geology Department of the University and contains the largest collection of minerals in the world—some twenty-five thousand species. These include precious, semiprecious, and other rare stones. Some of the stones are truly magnificent and make one appreciate the beauty of the inorganic natural world. We also admired some of the early machines used for extracting the minerals and toured a replica of the inside of a gold mine. We could thus appreciate the conditions under which those who worked in the mines, often slaves of African origin, had to live. In 1827 British engineers brought new machines to Minas Gerais, products of the ongoing industrial revolution in England, a revolution that had started in the middle of the eighteenth century. These machines helped initiate a mini industrial revolution in Minas Gerais.

After the visit to the mineral museum we had lunch at a restaurant called Degusta where we enjoyed Brazilian live music and tasted typical local foods such as fried pork skin, chicken cooked with coconut, various kinds of beans and others. After lunch we visited the Museum of the Oratory, a small museum that contains a superb collection of one hundred sixty-three oratories and three hundred sacred images from the last four centuries. A private collector named Angela Gutierrez donated the collection to the Brazilian government. Oratories are movable altars, some small enough to be carried in the pockets of the miners' coats and some too large to be easily moved.

Their basic function was to provide their owners, wherever they were, with the company and protection of Saints, the Madonna and Jesus. This protection was particularly important for those who worked so far from churches that they were unable to attend religious services. There were various categories of "oratorios," including:

> *(a) oratorio de viagem*, or *oratorio itinerantes*, is oratorio for travelers;
> *(b) oratorio bala*, in the shape of bullets;
> *(c) oratorio de salao*, for large living rooms or salons;
> *(d) oratorio de alcove*, for corners within houses;
> *(e) oratorio erudito* sophisticated oratorios; and
> *(f) oratorio de concha*, built like sea shells; and others.

The collection also contained some beautiful *ex votos, santos*, and other similar religious objects. These religious works were extraordinarily beautiful. Many reflected African influences because they had been produced by African slaves. Given the hundreds of thousands of people who were snatched from Africa and brought to the New World, one can clearly see the African influence in places like Ouro Preto.

After the visit to the Museum of the Oratory we visited two magnificent churches: the Church of Saõ Francisco and the Church of Our Lady of Pilar. Here we saw the extraordinary sculptural work by Antonio Francisco Lisboa, generally known as Aleijadinho, or the "Little Cripple." Aleijadinho was born in 1730, or some say 1733, and died in 1814, which was a long life span for his time. He was the illegitimate son of a successful Portuguese master carpenter and architect, Manuel Francisco Lisboa, and of an African slave. Because of his mother, legally, he was born a slave. His father had to buy his freedom when he was a young man. Crippled by a disease, he could not use his hands and needed to have the hammer and the chisel tied to his wrists when he worked on his sculptures. This made the process of carving stones extremely painful. Therefore he often used soft stone or wood for his sculptures. And what sculptures they were! In my humble opinion, I believe that if Aleijadinho had operated in Europe, he would be considered one of the world's outstanding sculptors. Unfortunately not many outside of Brazil are likely to have heard of him, although, as

I will mention later, UNESCO has recently recognized the outstanding quality of his work. I had heard of him only recently through the previously mentioned book by Fernandez-Armesto, *The Americas*.

We also visited the Church of Our Lady of Pilar built in 1711 and finished in 1732, before Aleijadinho's time. Because the church was built during the gold rush, it is the second richest in gold in Brazil, after the Church of Saõ Francisco, in Salvador de Bahia. It has about half the quantity of gold of the Saõ Francisco Church. Its style is pure Portuguese baroque and all its wood decorations are covered by gold leaf. These churches tend to be round and resemble a theatre.

In the evening we decided to have pizza at a pizzeria in Praça Tiradentes, so that we could see the procession that the major had mentioned. We assumed that it would pass in front of the pizzeria so we chose a table near the window. Due to rain, the procession began late, with fewer people following the statue of the Madonna than we had anticipated. A band followed the procession playing Brazilian baroque music. Speaking of music or sounds, I should add that during our two days' stay in Ouro Preto we enjoyed the constant tolling of the Church bells that, because of the echo created by the hills, had an almost celestial quality. It seemed as if it was the voice of God calling. This is a call that is rarely heard in modern metropolitan areas. Thus, when it is heard, it definitely makes one feel closer to the Almighty.

The next morning we visited the Museum of the Casa Dos Contos. It had been highly recommended to us by former minister Marcilio Moreira. The Casa dos Contos is a magnificent building that encapsulates a lot of the history of Minas Gerais and of Brazil. Its location offers great vistas of the city, especially from some of its upper windows. Built between 1782 and 1784 by a very rich man, João Rodriguez de Macedo, it served as his residence and as a *casa dos contratos*, or "house of contracts. The Casa dos Contos could be considered the equivalent of a modern tax collecting office. Another important figure in the building's history was Rodrigo de Macedo, a contract bidder of titles and other payments to the state. Titles were shares of production to be paid as taxes to the state and the church. At the time tax collecting was largely privatized, because official tax administrations had not yet been created. Rodrigo de Macedo was implicated in the "Inconfidencia Mineira," the act of rebellion against the Portuguese Crown that was largely a tax revolt spurred by high taxes. At that time, prominent Brazilians started to resent the taxes and the controls imposed by the Portuguese Crown. The previously mentioned Tiradentes had met with some of the conspirators within the Casa dos Contos. The Portuguese Viceroy sent a squadron to overtake the building and suppress the rebellion. The Casa dos Contos then became a prison for some of the conspirators, who were members of the nobility. Subsequently the Council of the Royal Treasury and the Gold Intendancy was transferred into the Casa dos Contos. In 1803, the Royal Treasury moved indefinitely into the building. In 1820, it was expanded to accommodate a Casa de Fundição de Ouro, or a gold foundry, which was largely operated by slaves. In 1844, the Secretariat of Provincial Finance and the Office of the Empire's Treasury moved into the building. After 1897, when Brazil became a republic, it was occupied by the Post Office and by the Federal Savings Bank. In 1973, it became a National Archive containing the microfilms of the country's important historical documents. It is now a haven for researchers. A book, *A Casa dos Contos de Ouro Preto,* by Eugenio Ferraz, provides a full history of this historically important building.

In the Casa dos Contos one can see the various moneys that have circulated in Brazil, especially those from recent decades. One can also appreciate the impact of inflation on the monetary unit. For example the Cruzeiro, introduced in 1942 with the image of Tiradentes on Cr$5000 and Santos Dumont on Cr$10,000, was replaced by the Cruzeiro Novo in 1967. In the process the Cruzeiro lost three zeros. The Cruzeiro Novo lasted three years and in 1970 was again replaced by the Cruzeiro losing only one zero. In 1986, the Cruzado replaced the Cruzeiro, again losing three zeros. Then just three years later, the Cruzado Novo (NCz$) replaced the Cruzado (Cz$), which lost four zeros this time. The Cruzado Novo had a short life. One year later, in 1990, it was replaced once again by the Cruzeiro, losing one zero in the process. The 1990 Cruzeiro lasted less than three years, and this time the surgery was more radical. It lost four zeros and was replaced by the Cruzeiro Real (CR$) which, just one year later, was replaced by the Real at the rate of fifty thousand to one. Fortunately, the Real has remained in existence up to now because Brazil was finally able to control inflation.

The history of Brazil's currency is a great lesson on what happens when governments pursue unrealistic economic policies. More specifically, this is what happens when governments spend more than they receive in ordinary revenues over a long period of time. This could be an important lesson for some industrial countries. Hopefully the Real (R$) will have a long life, and recent developments make this seem likely. Inflation has been contained so far, although in 2008 there was a minor pick-up in it.

The visit to Ouro Preto also marked a significant emotional, rather than intellectual, milestone for me. The experience forced me to reflect upon the institution of slavery and the role that it had played in the New World. Once I started thinking about it I could not shake the horrors of slavery from my mind. The fact that human beings were taken from their homes and shipped thousands of miles away, under horrible conditions, to be sold like cattle or machines, was terrible to imagine. It became difficult to comprehend how some of those engaged in this trade were citizens of countries that had advocated rule of law and the equality of all human beings. It has been estimated that the English shipped 2,360,200 slaves from Africa in the whole eighteenth century, part of a grand total of 5,513,300 slaves shipped in that century. The lucrative slave trade helped finance England's imperial expansion. For a fuller account of this, one should look at H.A. Gemery and Jan Hogendorn's "Evidence on English/African Terms of Trade in the Eighteenth Century," published in *Explorations in Economic History*. In Brazil, the children of slave mothers were born as slaves, regardless of who the father was, until the "Free Womb Law" of 1871 freed any children born after that date. The full abolition of slavery itself did not come until 1888.

After the visit to the Casa dos Contos, we left Ouro Preto for Congonhas do Campo, a small town on the way to Belo Horizontes where we would catch a return flight to Rio. When we left Ouro Preto, the clouds were covering large parts of the town so that some of the hills had disappeared behind them. All the while, the bells were still making their wonderful sounds. In addition, while we were leaving the hotel, we could hear Gregorian chants coming from the hotel conference room. This combination of sounds inevitably made one think of heaven.

Like Ouro Preto, Congonhas is another town that benefited enormously from both the gold rush and the work of Aleijadinho. It has about forty thousand inhabitants, or half the present size of Ouro Preto. The Basilica of the Good Lord Jesus (Bom Jesus de Matosinhos), surrounded by seventy-four Aleijadinho sculptures, has also become part of the UNESCO sites of importance to mankind. The Basilica is on a hill that dominates the town, and Aleijadinho worked there for eight years. His "Last Supper," located in one of the enclosed chapels, and the large stone statues of the twelve prophets, located in the open area in front of the church, are truly extraordinary.

About three hundred feet from the front of the church there are six stone chapels that enclose statues representing six stages of the Cross. They were also made by Aleijadinho. Unfortunately, the chapels are kept closed, and the statues can only be seen through a locked entrance door without the benefit of direct lighting. This makes it a bit difficult to fully appreciate the power and the beauty of these statues. The twelve prophets, on the other hand, are in the open, exposed to the weather and to vandals who, over three centuries, have left their marks on the statues. In spite of this, they remain as extraordinary as almost any work of art I have ever seen.

Aleijadinho worked in Congonhas a few years after the execution of Tiradentes. One of his statues of Jesus reproduces Tiradentes' features, even including blood around his neck. In this way, Aleijadinho reminds us of Tiradentes' beheading. The expressions on the faces of the biblical prophets are very powerful. The entire complex is worth a visit to Brazil and to Congonhas. We were told that there are plans to transfer the statues to a museum and replace them with replicas. However, due to lack of funds, this project has not been completed. The sooner it happens, the better it will be for Brazil and for mankind in general.

Before leaving the church complex, we visited the Sala dos Milagros, or the hall of miracles, a large room next to the church that contains thousands of ex votos. Ex votos are offers for miracles or favors received from God or from various protective saints, or for favors being asked from them. The room contains literally thousands of these ex votos, the largest and most diverse collection I had ever seen. The room also contained silver items, photographs, letters and paintings of particular miracles. Some of these objects were absolutely charming. My wife added to the collection by leaving photos of our grandchildren.

Ex votos are a unique expression of human faith and they have generated a distinct form of naïf art in various Latin American and European Catholic countries, as well as in the Philippines. They are common in Mexico, especially in the form of small paintings often painted on tin plates. I once saw an exhibition of them at the Palacio de Bellas Artes in Mexico. Alfredo Vilchis Roque and Pierre Schwartz have published a beautiful book on these unique artworks, entitled *Rue des Miracles*. I had seen very good collections at two churches in Italy, one in Torino and one in Bari. In the Basilica of Saint Nicholas in Bari, where the Saint's remains are buried, the ex votos take the form of painted bottles dedicated to the patron Saint.

After our visit to Minas Gerais we returned to Rio for a day. We decided to skip the traditional tourist part of the city and, in the religious mood inspired by Ouro Preto and Congonhas, we decided to visit some of Rio's famous churches. It was the Sunday before Easter, the perfect time for this kind of sightseeing. We visited three churches: the new Cathedral, the old Cathedral (the Candelaria), and São Bento Monastery. We also planned to visit Rio's museum of Naïf Art that was advertised as having the largest collection of such paintings in the world. We started with the new Cathedral.

Built like a steep pyramid, the Rio Cathedral was unlike most churches that we had seen. It was designed by Edward de Oliveira da Fonseco and is similar in style to the Cathedral in Brasília. However, the Rio Cathedral is much larger. The inside is a circle with a diameter of about 350 feet. It is estimated that the Cathedral can accommodate twenty thousand people. It is 315 feet high with the main door already reaching almost 60 feet. We visited the Cathedral on the Sunday morning before Easter, and there was the Palm Mass taking place, as well as singing and dancing. Despite the many people inside the church, it still was not full. Inside the church, we saw beautiful and immense stained glasses. Apart from the stained glass, the inside is somewhat bare and different from the churches we had seen in Ouro Preto or the ones we were going to see next. The second church we visited was the Candelaria, the first Cathedral built in Rio during the colonial period. It reflects the Portuguese style that predominated during the seventeenth century. Its magnificent iron doors depict various scenes with angels. In the front of the church, there is an impressive statue of a freed female slave, which was obviously added much later after the abolition of slavery. Two other impressive features of the church are the leather and wood chairs provided for the public, and the extraordinarily beautiful carvings on the stairways leading to two pulpits. The contrast between this cathedral and the newer one we had seen, built some three centuries later, showed the great gulf between tradition and modernity. A pertinent question is which of the two helps more to elevate the spirit towards the creator. I would have a hard time answering that question.

Finally, we visited the Monastery of São Bento and its fabulous church. We were advised that this church was not to be missed because it was the richest one in Rio. When we reached São Bento, mass had just ended, and the church was emptying. There were few people in the church so that we were able to visit it comfortably. Unlike the other two large churches that we had visited, this one was small. An extraordinary amount of gold had been used to cover the marvelous wood carvings in the church. Almost every square inch of the inside of the church was occupied by exquisitely- carved angels or by other religious figures, all painted in gold. We spent a lot of time admiring this marvelous expression of religious faith and tried to take some photos, although the amount of light in the church was limited. Before we left the church, a small group of monks came in and we had the pleasure of listening to their heavenly Gregorian chants, accompanied by the old church organ. When we left the church, the bells were again tolling. To us it seemed to be another call from Heaven, and we rushed to buy CDs of the São Bento Monastery's Gregorian Chants. I had been to Rio many times before and somehow I had come to mainly associate the city with the usual tourist attractions of Copacabana, Ipanema, Sugar Loaf, and the Cristo Redentor. Our visits to the churches made it clear to me that I had missed a vital dimension of Rio. It is a pity that many think of Rio as just a beach town.

My wife and I returned to Brazil a few weeks later, in May 2008. The International Association of Public Budget, ASIP, had invited me to speak at the "XXXV Seminario Internacional de Orçamento Público." It was held at the Brasília Alvorada Hotel, and I spoke on "The Role of the State and Public Finance" to an audience of a thousand people. I stressed the importance of making budgetary decisions not on the basis of labels (such as social spending, economic spending and so on) but on the basis of who actually benefits from the money spent and of actual results. I stressed that often spending does not benefit the intended beneficiaries but mainly those who deliver the services. The paper was well received and the organization decided to publish the paper on which my talk had been based. The inspiration for this paper came from the fact that several economists and public officials were pushing countries to increase "social spending," arguing that this would improve the income distribution of Latin American countries. The Millennium Goals established by the United Nations had also been interpreted as a call for increasing public spending in what were called social expenditure categories. There was not much concern over whether this spending would actually benefit the poor. My worry was that, through various kinds of leakages, this spending could become a subsidy to particular categories of middle class citizens, such as school administrators and teachers, nurses and doctors, and public employees that administer some of these programs. Little of the spending might actually reach the intended beneficiaries. I had some evidence from Chile (for public health spending) and from Mexico (for educational spending) that larger budgetary allocations to these categories of spending had not had any measurable effects on the patients and schoolchildren who were presumably the beneficiaries. In the cases of Chile and Mexico, the main change had been in the salaries of those who delivered the services.

My wife had never been to Brasília. Given her (and my) interest in photography we took advantage of the visit to take photos of the city's stunning buildings. We took photos of the Palace of Justice, the National Theatre, the National Library, the Cathedral, the President's residence (Palacio de Alvorada) and the Palacio Itamaraty. In these buildings, one can see Niemeyer's and other Brazilian architects' genius. We visited the inside of the Cathedral, which can be accessed through an underground passage. The cathedral is partly underground so that its vastness is not evident from the outside. The inside of the cathedral is very austere. There are only two sculptures: a copy of Michelangelo's Pietá, and a large crucifix. The altar is raised like a stage and sits in a circular area with fixed marble stools all around. A remarkable feature is the magnificent stained glasses that adorns a large part of the inside surface. We visited the inside of the Palacio Itamaraty, which serves as the ceremonial place for the Ministry of Foreign Affairs, inaugurated on April 21, 1970. The exterior is like a mirage because the building is surrounded by water and by beautiful water plants. The interior is remarkably tasteful. On the ground floor, a very large area without any apparent support for the ceiling, there is a breathtaking stone stairway in the middle that is shaped like a semicircle and leads to the floor above. The steps seem to be suspended in the air and to have no visible support. The building contains several works of art and a famous desk that has been used to sign important documents, including the law that freed the slaves in 1888. One of the important works of art on display is a painting of the coronation of Don Pedro Primero.

The day after the conference we made arrangements to visit Pirenópolis, a town located in the Brazilian state of Goiás about 90 miles from Brasília. The city is well-known for its small but beautiful waterfalls, for its well preserved colonial architecture, and for its popular Festa do Divino Espirito Santo, which takes place forty-five days after Easter. In this area it rains a lot for seven months, and then it hardly rains for five. The lack of rain and the very low (roughly twelve percent) humidity in the summer make the place very dry and susceptible to frequent fires. During the trip I learned something about the demand for land by landless peasants, who want land close to the cities and not in the middle of nowhere. At times these peasants refuse the land allocated to them by the government and engage in the illegal occupation of some private land. These actions inspire criticism that the government is not able to protect property rights. This seems to be an oft- heard criticism of the Lula government. I was told that the public demonstrations in favor of land redistribution are often organized by left-leaning unions that hire unemployed workers to demonstrate. Those who demonstrate are paid for their service, an example of the market at work. In turn land owners hire private guards to prevent squatting on their land. This represents the privatization of a service that should be provided by the state.

On the way to Pirénópolis we visited a private farm, Bonsucesso, in which there were several beautiful waterfalls. To get to the farm one has to drive for about three miles on a really bad dirt road. Once we got to the farm we had to pay an entrance fee and then climb a steep path up a mountain to get to the falls. The climb was difficult but it was worth it. We visited at least five different waterfalls. The water came straight out of the mountain and formed beautiful pools under the falls where a few people went swimming. We were slightly concerned to learn that the area was affected by yellow fever.

After our visit to the falls, we went to Pirénópolis where we discovered that the following day was the Festa do Divino Espirito Santo with its famous *cavalhadas*. In the *cavalhadas*, Moors fight Christians in a battle that lasts three days. They have been doing so since 1826, when Portuguese settlers brought the festival. Of course the Christians always win. We arrived on a Saturday, when the town was preparing for the festival. Various horsemen wearing papier-mâché helmets and very elaborate masks were going around scaring people. One could distinguish the Moors from the Christians form their colors: red for the Moors and blue for the Christians. The staged battle would be fought in a bullring and would involve many horses. Taking advantage of the situation, children were wearing masks, making noises, and asking for money. A big pile of wood, neatly stacked and rising to at least 20 feet, had been prepared next to the church Nossa Senhora de Rosario. It would be set on fire that evening.

Built in 1738, the church had been the main or only church in Central Brazil for a long time. It had burned down twice, the second time in the year 2000. Like many churches from that period, it is baroque in the typical Portuguese style, very simple outside and all white. The church has different sections for the rich and for the commoners. The slaves could not attend it so that another church, not far from this one, had been built for them. Slaves had no right to form families, although some slave owners encouraged their breeding so as to sell the offspring. This must surely have affected their concept of the family. This might explain why so many black families are still headed by women. Pirénópolis is a charming town that has been kept in its original eighteenth-century state. Strict regulations prevent any change in the historical part of the town, making the town charming and picturesque. It reminded us of Ouro Preto, although it is not quite as interesting. Most of the old houses have one of two types of particular decoration just under the roof tiles. The two types of decoration are called *eira* and *beira*. The houses of the rich had both kinds of decorations. Those of the middle classes generally had just one. Those of the poor did not have any. As a result, even today when a family is poor it is said that it has "neither *eira* nor *beira*," or in Portuguese it is a family "sen eira nen beira".

Over these many years and many trips, I came to see Brazil as an extremely interesting and beautiful country but one difficult to grasp in all its complexity and scope. I had the impression that the more I saw of it, the less I felt that I knew it. Its size, its diversity, and its beauty make it different from most other countries. When people think of Brazil, they tend to focus on only the dimension or the characteristic of it that interests them. Some think of the beaches. Some focus on the spectacular natural beauty of Rio de Janeiro. Some focus on the vastness and mystery of the Amazonian forests. Some are fascinated by the architectural marvels of Brasília. Few probably ever think of the historical areas and of the old churches that at times give one the impression of being in the middle of some old European town and not in the New World. This is a country that deserves many visits focused on different aspects of it. But it is too big to ever feel that one knows all of it.

In October 2009 the Olympic Committee chose Rio de Janeiro as the site for the 2016 Olympics This would be the first Olympic held in South America. Perhaps, after all, Brazilians will no longer wait for the future to arrive.

PART II

PERU AND CHILE

CHAPTER 6

PERU: EARTHQUAKE AND THE PISCO SOUR

I can still vividly recall my first visit to Peru in the late 1960s, even though so many years have passed. During this period, I was a professor of economics at the American University in Washington, while also working as a consultant for the Organization of American States (OAS). On behalf of the OAS, I went to Lima to assess the role of tax incentives in Peru's development. At that time, some economists and most policymakers were confident of the positive influences of tax incentives on economic development. After that trip, which also included visits to Colombia and Ecuador, I wrote a report for the OAS, and subsequently I extracted an article for a German economic journal, *Finanz-Archiv*. In the two texts, I took a highly skeptical position vis-à-vis the role of tax incentives. Later experiences and analyses did not change my views on this subject. I became convinced that a stable tax system, with low or moderate rates and simple administration, was the best incentive that a government could provide to investors and economic agents in general. However, tax incentives, including the ones in Peru, have continued to be popular even to this day, though they inevitably complicate tax systems, promote corruption and provide questionable benefits. Policymakers like to have incentives that allow them to provide favors to supporters.

Peru is a country rich in mineral resources, in tradition, and in culture. Its history goes back thousands of years. When the Europeans arrived, the country already had a large population. Today it has a population close to thirty million people. Many Peruvians speak Quechua, the language spoken at the time of the Spanish conquest, rather than the official language of Spanish. Many are direct descendents of the Incas or of other indigenous people. Many are *mestizo*, reflecting the mixing of various races that has taken place in the past five hundred years. In Peru, the conflicts between cultures have had a large impact on economic policy and political developments in general. The impact of this conflict is perhaps more visible here than in most Latin American countries, with the possible exceptions of Ecuador, Guatemala and Bolivia.

Peru was the center of the powerful Incan Empire, which stretched for thousands of miles from Argentina to Colombia, mostly along the Pacific coast of South America. It spanned a huge area, with such ecological diversity that made it possible for its inhabitants to develop many important crops. Before and during the time of the Incas, many highly developed civilizations inhabited the region. Unlike that of the Mayas, this civilization did not develop its own writing, so that whatever information we have is less detailed compared with the Maya. However, the Incas did record some important information through the use of a system of knots of different colors.

The Spanish conquered the Incan Empire between 1527 and 1533, making Peru the center of their colonial empire in the Americas. Peru was so highly prized by the Spanish that they began to use the expression "vale un Peru," or "it is worth a Peru," to describe something very valuable. The Incan and Spanish cultures have continued to coexist, though not always peacefully.

Despite the country's natural resources and its rich cultural background, the per capita income of Peru has remained relatively low. However, in recent years it has been growing at a faster pace. Furthermore, the total income of the country is distributed very unevenly. Its income distribution, measured by a statistic called the Gini Coefficient (after the name of an Italian statistician), is one of the most uneven in the world. The discrepancy usually falls along ethnic lines. In addition to Europeans and Incan descendants, the major ethnic groups include Japanese, Chinese, and Africans. The descendants of the Incas have the lowest income, while the descendants of the Europeans and of some other groups, such as the Japanese, have the highest incomes. Recently there has been little mixing among the groups, although those in the *mestizo* population continue to intermarry. There are sharp class distinctions among the population. Some of the old families who claim to descend from the Spanish conquerors have much of the wealth and the high social standing. Some of these families have established international links through marriages that make it easier for them to benefit from the growing globalization. Few ever marry individuals of other ethnic groups.

The different ethnic groups have created a rich multicultural environment, especially in Lima. This is reflected in the cuisine and in the music, and Peru has perhaps the richest cuisine in Latin America. The combination of local cuisines with the Chinese has created a particularly interesting variety called *chifa*, the Cantonese word for "to eat." The music also ranges from pure Andean to Afro-Peruvian.

In the 1960s, Lima was still a relatively safe city where one could walk around even at night at least in the historical center. When the workday ended in downtown Lima, one could walk to the crowded street called Calle de la Union and watch some extraordinarily beautiful girls go by. The uneven income distribution seemed to be reflected in the uneven distribution of looks among women. Here one could see truly beautiful and truly unattractive girls. Economic growth seems to reduce these differences in look but it does not necessarily increase the average look. At that time, the Hotel Bolivar was considered the best hotel, located right in the historical center in the beautiful Plaza de Armas and near Plaza San Martin. A lot of the social activity evolved around this hotel and this area.

Lima is located in a strange geographical area, essentially a desert valley. Due to the very cold Humboldt's current, which keeps the sea temperature near Lima at around 45 degrees Fahrenheit, the weather is relatively cool for much of the year despite the proximity to the Equator. It almost never rains, but there is often a kind of thick fog called *garua*, which feels like a very light rain and makes the place wet and humid. Sometimes weeks pass with hardly any sign of the sun; there is only the continuous dampness of the *garua*. The Limeños describe the sky during these periods as a "panza de burro," or donkey's belly. Due to the lack of rain, there are few trees in Lima and little greenery, except in the more prosperous parts of the city where one can afford irrigation. In these areas there has been an increase of greenery in recent years. Of course, cacti do well. It is puzzling why the Spanish Viceroyalty would have chosen this depressing geographical area for its capital. Most likely the reason was its proximity to a good harbor.

Lima's port area of Callao is a colorless and almost depressing sight. In recent decades, the development of the fishing industry in Callao attracted a lot of immigrants from the interior of the country and, because of the high unemployment, made the area less safe. Here the color of the ocean is a dark and sad grey, and the coastline, which is for the most part devoid of vegetation or color, seems to fall suddenly in the ocean. One has the impression that the dividing line between the land and the ocean is constantly shifting and that at any moment parts of the elevated coastline could suddenly fall into the sea.

During my first visit to Lima I was happy to see two friends from my earlier Harvard days. They were both economists: Richard Webb, who became President of the Central Bank of Peru, and Daniel Shydlowski, who became an advisor to the President of Peru. Their last names alone provide an example of the Peru's diversity. Over the years, I would occasionally run into them. Richard Webb would be the author of a major history of the World Bank. Shydlowski would spend many years in the US teaching economics in Boston and Washington, before going back to Peru.

One episode from that first visit has remained in my memory all these years because it is highly indicative of what civilization can do to human nature. One night I was waiting for a colleague, Jaime Cifuentes, an Ecuadorian who was traveling with me on the mission. He had gone to see a dentist because he was having painful toothaches. I sat in the lobby of the Hotel Crillon where we were staying. It was a downtown hotel not far from the Hotel Bolivar. It no longer exists. I ordered a *pisco sour*, the typical Peruvian drink that combines lime juice with *pisco*, a distillate of grape that is similar to the Italian *grappa*. The hotel lobby was a large area and at that hour it was crowded with many people. It was partly enclosed by large glass windows through which the street was clearly visible. The waiter delivered the drink and left the bill on the table in front of me. Suddenly, I felt a shaking of the ground that grew in intensity. The shaking reminded me of my childhood when I would walk near the railroad tracks in my hometown in Italy and wait for the fast trains that went by without stopping.

As the shaking intensified, the people in the crowded lobby stood up and rushed for the exit. It took me several seconds to realize what was happening. It was an earthquake and a relatively powerful one. At that moment, I also got up to rush outside, but then something clicked in my brain and made me stop: I realized that I had not paid my bill! How could I leave without having paid for the *pisco sour*? After a moment of hesitation I sat down and some seconds later, the shaking of the ground stopped. The people slowly came back in. Many looked pale. Sometime later, my colleague arrived, and Webb came to pick us up for dinner. He said that his legs felt like rubber because of the fear that earthquakes bring to people who live in earthquake areas. Lima is situated in a seismic area so that earthquakes are rather common. Webb was amused when I told him how I reacted to the earthquake, and we both attributed it to a fundamental corruption of human nature. When paying a small bill becomes more important than protecting one's life, something must be terribly wrong. This was one of three times I would be in an earthquake. Fortunately, in all three cases (Lima, New Delhi, and San Jose in Costa Rica), my immediate area was not damaged, although other parts of those cities suffered heavy damages. In Lima and New Delhi, some people were hurt or even killed. In developing countries, even earthquakes seem to make a distinction between low- and high- income areas and people.

The years after my first visit were not good for Peru. Over the next three decades its per capita income went down rather than up and economic conditions worsened as did the security situation. A fanatical Maoist movement called Sendero Luminoso (the lighted path) started a campaign of terrorism, kidnapping, and killing. This movement, led by mysterious leaders, including a former academic Abimael Guzman, exploited the widespread resentment against ethnic whites and against those who belonged to the higher classes and the government. Over the years it contributed to the death of some sixty-nine thousand people who were either killed by the terrorists or in crossfire with governmental forces.

Peru's economic decline accelerated during the Alan García administration, the so-called lost decade of the 1980s. García was a devout populist with far left ideas. He was contemptuous of the market economy and impatient with market principles even though, to be fair, he had inherited a difficult situation in a difficult period. This period coincided with the debt crisis and the rise of the drug economy in which narcotraffic and narcodollars became widespread. Inflation accelerated and the ratio of total taxes to GDP (the tax burden) fell to as low as seven percent. The government tried to get additional resources for its needs by printing money and by borrowing from foreign sources including the IMF. The net result was hyperinflation and the accumulation of a huge foreign debt that the government was soon unable to service. By the end of the 1980s, Peru was in arrears to the Fund by about one billion dollars. At that time that was a huge amount. The Fund stopped lending to Peru and, because of the arrears, it cut most relations with the Peruvian government.

The leftist rhetoric and the populist policies of Alan García did not help. Incomes kept falling, prices kept going up, and the infrastructure became dilapidated due to lack of operation and maintenance expenditure. The country, and Lima in particular, became perhaps the most unsafe places in Latin America. The beautiful, historical center of Lima was largely abandoned and the hotels there, including the Bolivar and the Crillon, were forced to close down. The University of San Marco, one of the oldest Universities in the Americas was taken over by leftists and its academic standards collapsed. In addition to narcotraffic, another booming industry was that of bodyguards to protect homes, shops, offices, and movements on roads. Kidnapping became common. One could not venture around Lima at night because of the danger of being robbed and also because the government had imposed a curfew in the hope of reducing crime and terrorism. During these years there were several episodes of terrorist bombing with tragic consequences.

One popular joke from that time conveys some sense of how bad the situation had become. The story goes that President García and President George H. Bush die together in an accident and are both received by the Devil in the warm waiting room of Hell. The Devil tells the two presidents that, despite his bad reputation, he is quite a fair guy. Therefore, in light of the two presidents' importance, he will allow them to argue their case for which level of Hell they are to be assigned. Of course, the deeper the level, the hotter and less comfortable Hell becomes. The Devil adds that they can choose a lawyer to argue their cases. Of course García's lawyer is in Lima and Bush's is in Texas. The Devil invites the two presidents to use Hell's public telephone to make the call to their respective lawyers. However, he explains that they have to pay for the phone calls because Hell, like so many other places, is having budgetary problems at that time because of increasing costs and falling revenue. García decides to call first. He deposits the required quarter and makes the call. Bush follows but he is told by the Devil that his call will cost not a quarter, but fifty dollars. When the president complains about the discriminatory treatment and asks for an explanation, the Devil explains simply that García's was a local call, one from Hell to Hell!

I went back to Peru in December 1990, immediately after the election of President Fujimori. Fujimori had won a surprise election. Up to that time he had been an obscure agricultural expert without any apparent political base. His election had originally been seen as a kind of joke, or, at most, as a protest vote. In a different way it was an extraordinary sign of globalization: an individual of Japanese descent taking over the government of a country that had been the heart of the Incan Empire!

On this trip I was again accompanied by my IMF colleague Partho Shome, the Indian economist that had accompanied me in Brazil. At this time Peru was undergoing its worst economic crisis in a long time. The economic situation had deteriorated considerably. Inflation had gone through the roof. A simple dinner in a normal restaurant cost the two of us forty million soles! The government was broke, and the country was not servicing its debt. It had become an international pariah and was not getting any loans from the IMF or from other international sources. Meanwhile its debt continued to increase because of unpaid interest.

If the economic situation was bad, the security situation was worse. The Sendero Luminoso controlled much of the country, and the government seemed to control only portions of Lima. Car bombings were frequent and often damaged buildings including embassies. The Sendero Luminoso frequently damaged power plants, leaving Lima in the dark for days. To make matters worse, at that time there was a serious outbreak of cholera. The government seemed unable to do much because tax collection had collapsed and nobody was willing to lend it any money. In many areas, government presence had literally disappeared, and for many citizens, Lima was pretty close to a Hell on Earth. It was definitely not a place that one would want to visit at that time.

My trip was in response to an invitation from the newly appointed Minister of Finance, who was also the Prime Minister. At the time, because of the large arrears in its debt servicing towards the IMF, the Fund was not allowed to have financial dealings with this country. It could not even provide technical assistance. However, now that a new government was in place, it was felt that the Fund should try to reestablish contacts and help Peru to reenter the world of economic legitimacy. An exploratory, technical-assistance mission was a way of reestablishing these contacts. In time, a clever piece of financial engineering helped solve the problem created by the country's unpaid debt to the Fund. Simply put, a deal was made to have some countries, mainly Spain, lend money to Peru. This money was immediately used to clear the arrears with the Fund. This in turn made it possible for the Fund to lend new money to Peru so that Peru could repay the loan that it had just received from the other countries. In this way, Peru sidestepped the rule preventing the Fund from lending to countries in arrears, and the Fund could lend again to Peru provided that the latter made needed reforms.

Shome and I paid our first visit to the Prime Minister. When we got to his office at the Ministry of Finance, we had to make our way through some angry demonstrators. As it turned out, these demonstrators were schoolteachers who had not been paid for months, during which rampant inflation had dramatically cut the real value of their salaries. Once we got through the demonstrators and entered the building, we discovered that the elevators were not working and that the Minister's office was on the eighth floor. We had no choice but to use the stairs. There we discovered that the stairs were cluttered with supplies and with construction material for some urgent repairs. I could not fail to think of the possibility of earthquakes.

After some difficulties, and a bit out of breath, we eventually made it to the eighth floor and to the Minister's office. The Minister,

Hurtado Miller, was a tall, handsome, and sophisticated person. Given his look and his background people often compared him with Fujimori. These comparisons were not complimentary for the newly appointed president, who came from a modest background, was short, undistinguished, and, furthermore, was Japanese.

The Minister explained that the country had a major revenue problem. Simply put, its tax revenue had collapsed, and the government was not able to meet even the most basic needs, such as paying the past salaries of those protesting schoolteachers we had seen or making essential repairs to the decaying infrastructure. To replace the lost revenue from taxes, it had resorted to printing money, which had produced a hyperinflation. The hyperinflation, in turn through the "Tanzi effect," had contributed to the revenue collapse. Because of its arrears on the debt servicing, it could not borrow internationally. Minister Miller explained that he had appointed a commission to propose a tax reform and that this commission had already drafted some recommendations. He gave us a copy of the report. I promised that we would look at the commission's recommendations and give him a reaction that would be an informal Fund reaction. Although Minister Miller did not mention it, we learned that the chairman of the tax commission was one of his relatives.

The commission's recommendations were radical, to say the least. In a country with the very low tax burden (the ratio of total taxes to GDP) of about seven percent, the commission was recommending that these low tax rates be slashed and that all sorts of deductions and tax incentives be introduced! Perhaps an editorial in the *Wall Street Journal* would have endorsed this, since especially at that time the paper seemed to believe that cutting taxes was always the magical medicine for a sick economy. Unfortunately, cutting tax rates would not reduce inflation nor provide the government with the badly needed resources for essential public spending. To approve of this tax cut, one would have to believe in an extreme version of what was called the "Laffer curve." The Laffer curve argued that cutting tax rates when they were high increased tax revenue. This theory had made its appearance a few years earlier during the first Reagan administration. It was named after Arthur Laffer, a conservative economist, who once had used his napkin, at a luncheon with an American congressman, to explain graphically how cutting tax rates could raise tax revenue. The graph on the napkin had become famous in economics.

I wrote a memorandum to the minister bluntly telling him what I thought of the recommendations, that is, not much. The Minister was not happy with the message, but he could not ignore it because of the new government's strong desire to reestablish good relations with the IMF. True to form, the *Wall Street Journal* learned about this and sharply criticized the IMF for recommending tax increases to Peru. At the same time the *Wall Street Journal*, along with Alan Walters, the economic adviser to Margaret Thatcher, were criticizing the Fund for recommending that Russia raises taxes to close its large and growing fiscal gap. When I returned to Washington, I wrote an op-ed in which I criticized the paper's position, showing how absurd it was vis-à-vis the current economic circumstances of Peru and Russia. To its credit, the *Wall Street Journal* published my article with the catchy title "The IMF Strikes Back!" This exchange was somewhat ironic because some of the more devout supply-siders of the early 1980s had referred to my first book, *Personal Income Tax and Economic Growth*, published by Johns Hopkins University Press in support of their thesis. My book had argued that some major countries might have reduced their growth rate by imposing high personal income taxes.

A short time after this visit, Minister Miller left the government and the Fujimori administration began addressing the problem of extremely low tax revenue. The government invited the Fiscal Affairs Department of the IMF to help it raise badly needed revenue. It soon became obvious that part of the problem was a totally inefficient and corrupt tax administration. Our evaluation of the tax administration concluded that it was just too corrupt to be reformed. What was needed was truly radical surgery. It was necessary to shut down the existing tax administration, sending home most of its employees, and to create a new one from scratch. This new administration would have a salary structure comparable with that of the Central Bank, but the employees would not have tenure and could be fired at any sign of corruption or incompetence. Most of the new tax administration's staff was made up of recent university graduates. They had to take courses on ethics and on the importance of true professionalism. Furthermore, they were paid good salaries based on the assumption that low salaries encourage corrupt practices. Some of the senior staff came from the Central Bank.

On the Fund side, a tough and competent Chilean lady named Milka Casanegra coordinated much of the technical assistance. In another innovation, the new tax administration was to be financed by a share of the tax revenue that it collected. It could use this share in ways that it deemed appropriate. Thus, an incentive to perform was combined with administrative flexibility and full accountability. Survey techniques were developed to try to identify behavior, on the part of the administrators, that smelled of corruption.

Within a short time, the fiscal situation began improving significantly, and the new tax administration, SUNAT (Superintendencia Nacional de Tributacion), was able to move into a new building. Sendero Luminoso, the terrorist organization, became aware of SUNAT's success and paid it the ultimate compliment: it bombed it. Nevertheless, tax revenue started going up and, aided by the fall in inflation and by the fact that the economy started to grow rapidly, it soon reached twelve percent of GDP. This was still a low level by international standards but it was almost twice as high as it had been in the final years of the García administration. Some tax opponents started arguing that the true tax burden was higher because GDP was overestimated, thus lowering the ratio of taxes to GDP.

During the García period, the already highly regulated Peruvian economy had become greatly overregulated. Hernando De Soto, a Peruvian who for a while had been an advisor to Fujimori, wrote a book, *El Otro Sendero*, or *The Other Path*. His book showed how costly, in terms of both time and money, it was to initiate any new activity, such as opening a shop or a small enterprise, in Peru. These regulations discouraged new economic activity and sent many activities toward the underground or the informal economy. Thus, the informal economy boomed while the official economy stagnated. De Soto's book attracted a lot of attention in a period when the underground economy had become a lively topic for research and for journalistic writing.

At the time I had written several papers on the underground economy including one that suggested an econometric way of measuring its size as I reported in the section on Brazil. De Soto submitted an article on this topic to a professional journal, and it was sent to me to referee. I recommended that the journal accept the article. In later years De Soto added another twist to his thesis. In another book, *The Mystery of Capital*, he argued that the capital accumulated in the underground or informal economy may have a high value, but it is not productive. The reason is that, due to the lack of clear property title, it cannot be used as collateral to get credit for legitimate business ventures. De Soto believes that the use of credit is essential to growth. He describes the people who engage in the underground economy: "they have houses but not titles, crops but not seeds, businesses but not statutes of incorporation." Unfortunately, there may be some problems with De Soto's thesis, apart from his high estimates of the value of capital in the informal economy that have been challenged by some economists. Simply put, registering properties makes their owners liable to property taxes, thus discouraging them from applying for a formal recognition of their property titles. In 2004 De Soto won the "Milton Friedman-Prize for Advancing Liberty," given by the Cato Institute in Washington.

When I went to Peru in December 1990, I had just returned from a trip to Romania, where the Ceausescu's regime had abruptly come to an end just weeks before. The obvious contrast between Bucharest and Lima typified the differences between a vital, even though distorted, market economy and a sluggish, centrally-planned economy. Lima's sidewalks were cluttered with goods for sale, while Bucharest was characterized by absolute scarcity. The most depressing sight in Romania at that time was that of absolutely empty shelves in the shops. In Lima you could buy almost anything off the sidewalks: food, clothes, perfumes, typewriters, even refrigerators. These were all supposedly produced with the help of tax incentives and without paying taxes. In Bucharest on the other hand, hundreds of people would get in line whenever a truck stopped in front of a shop. They assumed that the truck was bringing something to buy and, in an economy of scarcity, people needed almost everything. Thus, I concluded that even a poorly working market economy, as undoubtedly was the Peruvian economy at that time, produces more consumer goods than a planned economy.

The few days that I spent in Lima were characterized mostly by the evaluation of the report of the tax commission. My colleague and I had some meetings with experts from the World Bank who had come to Lima to also establish contacts with the new administration. There were forty-eight of them. When I returned to Washington and reported to the Managing Director of the Fund, Michel Camdessus, that against two Fund members there were forty-eight World Bank members, he remarked that this was the right proportion! We paid a brief visit to the Archeological Museum which was void of people but full of beautiful works in terracotta, gold, textiles, and old weapons. I thought that the gold pieces and the terracotta (called *huacos*), produced by civilizations such as the Mochica and the Nazca, were among the most beautiful I had ever seen. They had nothing to envy to the best European works.

During our stay in Lima we had a constant concern for our personal safety. Unfortunately, this limited my search of old keys and locks, which I had been collecting for some time. However, I managed to get two nice colonial keys from an antique shop near the hotel. On the evening of our departure, Partho Shome and I lined up in front of the cashier at our hotel. The hotel was located in an area of Lima called Miraflores, an area considered very good. There was a short line, with a gentleman at the front and two other persons between him and us. The man in front had a square attaché briefcase that he had placed on the floor next to him while he inspected the hotel bill. When he had completed his brief inspection of the bill and reached for the briefcase, he discovered that it had disappeared. The two persons who had been between him and us had also disappeared. All this happened in a few seconds during which my colleague and I had been distracted by someone or something. The gentleman, a foreigner, had everything in his briefcase: money, credit cards, passport, plane tickets, and so on. One can imagine the difficulties that he would face in the next few days. For a while he could not believe what had happened, then, when the reality dawned on him, he looked desperate. Remarkably, all this had happened in front of us without our noticing anything.

After settling our account, we ordered a taxi from the hotel and the hotel personnel insisted that we travel to the airport with an armed escort. At the airport, while waiting for the plane, we could not fail to notice the number of foreign and mostly American or European looking women with very small children who often looked darker than them. At that time, Peru had become a major exporter of children for adoption. It seems that this kind of export flourishes during periods of poor economic activity. It is definitely a countercyclical activity.

CHAPTER 7

PERU: A VISIT TO MACHU PICCHU

In October 1995, I returned to Peru. The International Fiscal Association (IFA), SUNAT, and the Association of Entrepreneurs of Peru had invited me to be the first speaker at a conference at the Universidad de Lima. I took my first son, Vito Luigi, with me, and we had a difficult time getting to Lima. We were supposed to fly from Washington (Dulles Airport) to Lima via New York. However, there was a big storm in New York, and when we checked in with American Airlines at Dulles, we were told that it was going to be two hours late and that we would miss our connection to Lima. We then rushed to the other Washington Airport (then National now Reagan Airport) and arrived just in time for a TWA flight to New York. But by the time we arrived to check-in with Lan Chile in New York, it was too late. We then changed to a United Airlines flight to Miami, but we could not find our suitcases. We flew from Miami to Lima where we arrived at 5:00 am without the suitcases. They would arrive two days later. I managed to sleep for a couple of hours and then called Carlos Gallegos, a Fund fiscal expert who was working in Lima. We spent a good part of the day with him, trying to buy a shirt and a decent slack so that I could have some half-decent attire for my conference presentation the next day.

We also managed to visit the Gold Museum and the New National Art Museum. The building where the New National Art Museum was housed was originally built by the Ministry of Fishing in the 1960s and 1970s, when Peru was earning a lot of foreign exchange from the high demand for fishmeal. When fishing lost its importance, because of overexploitation of the fishing areas, the building became a museum. During those heydays of the fishing industry, a Peruvian of Italian origin, Luis Banchero, had made a vast fortune as the king of fishmeal. He was one of a small group of Italians who had been very successful in activities related to jewelry, ice cream, and chocolates, among other things. The building is enormous, with bats that fly freely and scare the visitors, and fantastic pieces of terracotta from all leading Peruvian cultures. At that time it also contained a recently discovered tomb of an Incan prince who had been buried with lots of gold and beautiful ceramics. He was referred to as the Peruvian Tutankhamen. The Gold Museum is a smaller building; it is very crowded and enormously rich. Its collection includes gold, silver, antique textiles, and *huacos*, which are old, terracotta figures and objects. It also has a lot of erotic potteries that leave little to the imagination. Some of these even depicted group sex scenes. Some depict obviously homosexual encounters and some even scenes of sex with animals.

The objects in both museums show the tremendous artistic ability of these peoples. It would be difficult to find works in any culture which surpass those produced by the Nasca or the Mochica, cultures that developed north and south of Lima centuries before the Incas. One may have heard of Nasca lines, named after the Nasca civilization. These are figures that extend for miles, are hundreds of feet wide and, can only be seen from the air. It is quite remarkable that they have survived thousands of years without disappearing, in part due to the dry conditions of the area where they are located. All sorts of theories have developed about these extraordinary lines, for example that they were landing strips for alien spacecrafts. In any case, it is difficult to imagine how they were made and what function they served.

We also visited the Cathedral of Lima, an interesting building with fake wood columns serving a purely esthetic function. Due to the earthquakes in the region, these columns do not actually support any of the building's weight. Francisco Pizarro, the illiterate conquistador from Estremadura in Spain, is buried here in the Plaza San Martin. In 1531, Pizarro and a small band of seasoned Spanish adventurers in search of fame and riches arrived in the Inca territory. Between 1531 and 1533, they were able to defeat the powerful Incan army, an army that had conquered much of the Pacific side of South America. The Incan Empire, Tawantinsuyo or Teohua-ntin-suyu, "the Land of the Four Sections" with the city of Cuzco at its center, dominated an immense territory through its powerful army. How Pizarro and his small band could prevail over that army is one of the great historical mysteries. Several elements seem to have played a role: guns, horses, protective armor, and, perhaps most importantly, internal divisions within the Incan Empire. The Incas had never seen guns and horses. It was probably a terrifying sight: bearded men covered in shining metal, sitting tall on these never-seen-before animals and making loud noises with guns that reminded the Incas of thunder and lightning. Incan weapons did not have the power to penetrate the metallic armor of the Spaniards. The diseases, brought by the Spanish and against which the local populations did not have immunity, probably finished off the job.

The exhaustion following a civil war probably facilitated the conquest of Peru. Before the arrival of Pizarro and his band, the powerful Emperor Huayna Capac had died. His two sons, Huascar and Atahualpa, had to share the empire and went to war to determine the succession. The war had resulted in much destruction and in tens of thousands of casualties. It had also made some previously conquered people less willing to accept their subordination to the Incas. In time Atahualpa emerged victorious, but he had won a much- weakened empire.

When Pizarro arrived, Atahualpa seemed willing, perhaps out of curiosity, to meet him. They met at Cajamarca on November 15, 1532. Atahualpa came accompanied by several thousands of mostly unarmed escorts while Pizarro was accompanied by his small but heavily armed companions. At the November 15 meeting, Atahualpa, unlike his subordinates, showed no fear of the horses during a demonstration by Hernando de Soto intended to impress or scare the Incas. The morning of November 16, Friar Vicente de Valverde accompanied Pizarro. Employing an interpreter and a Bible, the Friar attempted to instantly convert the Incan Emperor to Catholicism and subordinate him to the King of Spain. The Emperor had never seen a book and he had obvious difficulty in understanding what the Bible was. The Emperor showed little interest in the friar's confusing religious sermon, much of it must have been lost in translation. He reacted to the idea that he was a vassal of King Charles I, of whom he had never heard. Furthermore, he threw the Bible to the ground, and Pizarro used this as an excuse to attack the Atahualpa's mostly unarmed escorts. They were entrapped within the square that had only two small exits. This resulted in the massacre of Cajamarca, where thousands of Incas were killed, and the Emperor Atahualpa captured. Given that Incan society was vertically organized, the Emperor's capture left his soldiers without a clear center of command.

While a prisoner, Atahualpa offered to fill a large room with gold and precious stones in exchange for his release. Pizarro accepted the offer and, over the following months, the gold started piling up and filled a whole room. But then, to facilitate his conquest, Pizarro reneged on his promise and had Atahualpa killed on July 26, 1533. This led to decades of hostility between the Spanish and the followers of Atahualpa. Good descriptions of these events can be found in two books: *Fall of the Inca Empire*, by Philip Ainsworth Means and, for a more recent and more updated account, *The Last Days of the Incas*, by Kim MacQuarrie. These two books are highly readable. There are obviously many other books that describe these events.

Approximately five hundred people attended the conference in Lima on October 22. The entrepreneurs at the conference wanted lower tax rates, even though interest income and dividends were tax free, the corporate income tax rate was a normal thirty percent, and most individuals who paid *any* income taxes (less than two percent of the population) paid only fifteen percent on their taxable income. The entrepreneurs were particularly upset with a minimum tax on the estimated value of the assets of enterprises. This tax had been introduced to get some tax contributions from enterprises that seemed to escape paying anything. Some enterprises argued that they never made profits and thus could not afford paying the minimum tax. How they remained in business without ever making profits was not explained.

In my presentation, I defended the minimum tax and argued for a higher average tax ratio for Peru. At that time the ratio of taxes to

GDP was still only twelve percent, according to the official statistics, and I argued that this was too low to allow the state to perform its essential functions. It was one of the lowest tax ratios in the world. I also advocated some punishment for tax evaders suggesting, jokingly, that tax evaders should be hanged by their feet in the main square! But, I added, this should happen with a probability approaching zero. I was thus joking using the essence of some economic theory, developed by economists Michael Allingham and Agnar Sandmo, that was popular with public finance economists. My presentation was welcomed by the government but hated by the entrepreneurs. For them I became something of a *persona non grata*, and the next day some newspaper articles reported that the IMF wanted to hang tax evaders! In future years, other newspaper articles sometimes referred to me as the guy who wanted to hang tax evaders.

The day after the conference, my son and I flew to Cuzco to join a tour for which we had signed up. When we landed at the airport of Cuzco we found representatives from SUNAT and from the Central Bank waiting for us. This was in addition to the tour guide that we had hired from Lima. There was a clear embarrassment of riches. We told the tour guide that we would join the tour the next day so that we could spend the day with the official hosts. The problem was that, rather than split the day up between our two official hosts, each of them wanted us for the full day. After some negotiations, they agreed that we would spend up to 3:00 p.m. with the Central Bank's representatives and the rest of the day with the SUNAT's representatives. It was not an ideal solution for us but it solved a diplomatic problem.

When checking in to the Hotel Libertador, we were given drinks of coca tea, which is supposed to be good for our altitude of 11,500 ft. Some people are much affected by the high altitude of Cuzco and develop strong headaches or even faint. Fortunately, my son and I did not have any problem with it. The Hotel Libertador is charming with a good display of pre-Colombian ceramics and with the typically Peruvian ornate mirrors and paintings from the colonial period. It is located in front of the beautiful church of Santo Domingo that has a splendid bell tower. Cuzco was the capital of the Inca empire, which extended from Colombia to Argentina. It has many extraordinary monuments and ruins. It is also a beautiful city of four hundred thousand people today. It rests in a valley that was probably a lake thousands of years ago. The Spanish city was built on top of the Incan city and Spanish churches on top of Incan temples. This was a way of affirming who was the boss! The Spaniards were largely urban people so that the cities they built followed clear plans, just like Roman cities. Cuzco's city plan reflects this geometric order.

The Central Bank provided a car, actually a pick-up truck, with a driver and a guide, Anamaria, who was a charming and cultured Peruvian lady. We immediately set out for the Valle Sagrata, or the Sacred Valley. The drive is beautiful, with lots of exotic roads and rural scenes. We went by large mountains, some covered with glaciers. The road had a lot of potholes but it was generally passable. Unlike Lima, the vegetation here is luxuriant. For a dilettante photographer like me, it was paradise. We stopped frequently to take photos of natural scenes and local people. It seemed as if not much had changed since the time of the Incas. Wheels were still rare except for the occasional buses and, I suspect, so was the use of money. These were the two missing ingredients from the Incan Empire: wheels and money. It would be difficult to imagine our modern world without wheels or money. At the time of the Incas, exchanges were made through barter, and they depended more on the volume of the goods exchanged than on their value. Anyway the number of products exchanged must not have been too high. Gold and silver were used only for ornaments; they did not have a monetary value. This explains the natives' puzzlement at the Spanish conquerors' great interest in gold and silver.

The Valle Sagrata is a rich agricultural area with a pleasant climate. It was an area preferred by the Inca emperors and many important ruins are located in this area. We visited the Inca ruins of Tampumachay. We stopped at a colorful local market where I bought an Incan weapon, a metallic weapon with a handle that could be used to hit enemies on the head. There were lots of interesting things to buy in this market but unfortunately we were much constrained for time because we were expected to be back in Cuzco by 3 p.m. and delivered to the SUNAT people. Anamaria, the guide, was very well-informed on the history of the area and spoke beautiful Spanish. We much enjoyed listening to her. She told us a lot about the area and about the Incan Empire.

We were back at the hotel by 3:15 and were picked up by Rosario Miranda, another charming Cusqueña and a member of SUNAT. We went straight to the fortress of Sacsayhuaman, which is jokingly referred to as "sexy woman." This impressive ruin compares, at least in size, with almost anything I have seen anywhere. The stones used to build the fortress are gigantic, some as tall and wide as 12 feet. They are perfectly fitted, a process which in some instances involved twelve angles. How this was done remains a mystery. How did they cut these stones? How did they move them? I found this fortress almost as impressive as the pyramids. We spent a lot of time here and I again took many pictures. I just did not want to leave the place. The extra time spent here unfortunately reduced the time in Cuzco itself. In Cuzco we briefly visited the Plaza de Armas with the impressive cathedral and a few other places such as Koricancha Templo del Sol and the Jesuit church, La Compañia. Cuzco reminded me of Quito with similar setting, colors, and folklore. Fortunately, I would have another opportunity to return in early 2008.

Back at the hotel we had a spectacular dinner at the buffet prepared by the hotel restaurant. But before that we helped ourselves to some coca tea, a drink much resembling green tea. The next morning we had to wake up at 4:45 in order to be ready for our train for Machu Picchu. The train station was in the middle of a large and crowded local market. The train moved on narrow rail tracks and was relatively small. On the train we had assigned seats in the front wagon. That allowed us a very good view of the panorama as the train moved forward. Once out of Cuzco the train had to climb about 1500 feet before descending again. To make the climb possible the technique used was that of mountain roads which zigzag their way up so as to reduce the steepness of the climb. It is the same technique used by skiers to go down steep hills. The difference is that a train cannot make sharp turns. Therefore, it moved forward on one track and then it backed up into another track to move once again forward on still another one. Through a series of such maneuvers, it managed to climb to the needed height before it could start its trip toward Machu Picchu.

The ride from Cuzco to Machu Picchu is one of the most spectacular rides one can experience. The track mostly follows a deep valley or canyon through which a river flows. Toward Machu Picchu, the train moves in the same direction as the water because Machu Picchu is almost 3000 feet lower than Cuzco. The view of the mountains is spectacular, with some of them capped by glaciers. Cliffs succeed cliffs, and the view of agricultural terraces built by the Incas on the sides of steep mountains is breathtaking. The train crosses a few villages so that one can catch a glimpse of local life. This can create occasional problems because there is hardly any separation of the tracks from the fields. We evidenced this problem when, at a given moment, out of nowhere, three cows tried to cross the tracks while the train was advancing. Two were hit and, I suppose, they must have been killed. This accident must have significantly changed the wealth of some native family or families. The train did not stop but continued towards its destination. We arrived at about 10:00 a.m., or four hours after departure from Cuzco. This was the fast tourist train that makes only one scheduled stop. It has to share the single track with a local train that makes many stops and is even slower. Still, the average speed of our train was about fifteen miles an hour.

The train station at Machu Picchu is literally a hole in the middle of huge mountains. The village where the train stops is called Aguas Caliente (hot waters). The canyon through which the river flows and which follows the train tracks is particularly narrow at that point. The little space outside the station was crowded by street vendors who were peddling their local wares, sweaters, blankets, artisan products, etc.

In 1995 there were only two significant hotels at Machu Picchu. One was in the canyon at Aguas Caliente, the name of which derives from an old spa with hot springs believed to have magical, curative powers. These springs had been used by the Incan emperors and by other aristocrats in the past. Shirley MacLaine, the actress, had visited these hot springs a few years earlier when she had made a well-publicized visit to Machu Picchu. She reported on this trip in one of her books. The hotel in Aguas Caliente was about half an hour by bus from Machu Picchu itself. The other hotel was only about 100 feet from the entrance to the ruins of Machu Picchu. It was 1500 feet straight up above the railroad station at Aguas Caliente. To get there, one had to take a bus that literally climbed the mountain on an unpaved road without rails and which became muddy and slippery after the rains. This road was not for the faint of heart or for those who suffered from a fear of heights.

To get to Machu Picchu, and climb the 1500 feet, the buses used the same technique as the train except that, in their zigzagging, they had to keep moving forward. During the sharp turns the drivers of the upward-bound buses could not see whether a bus was coming down. As one looked straight down from the side of the bus, one could see the train station and the train below becoming progressively smaller. Seen from the station below, the bus looked like a fly climbing a wall. One got the impression that the bus was defying the law of gravity as it managed to get to the top in about thirty minutes.

Once it had reached the top, the bus stopped in front of the hotel. In 1995 the hotel was basic but comfortable and clean. More importantly, its position is incredibly convenient. It would be upgraded in later years and its restaurant expanded to accommodate large tour groups. Without even checking in, we left our bags with the hotel staff and joined an organized tour. The group crossed the ticket counter and moved toward the entrance between two large natural stones. Before one crossed the ticket counter there was still no sight of Machu Picchu so that one did not have any idea of what would appear on the other side of the entrance.

Machu Picchu appears in all its mystique and beauty only after one has crossed the narrow tunnel-like entrance. It is truly one of the most breathtaking views in the world; no wonder it is now considered one of the true Wonders of the World. Since one cannot satisfactorily describe the natural setting of Machu Picchu, perhaps it is best to think of a traditional opera house in which the balconies are huge mountains, reaching 18000 feet and where the stage is the place where the ruins of Machu Picchu itself rest. A canyon surrounds Machu Picchu on the right and left sides, and at the back of it there is a steep but not too tall mountain that provides a background to the stage. One can climb this mountain by an ancient, steep and narrow path that ends at the top where there is an ancient ruin. Incredibly, there are also some agricultural terraces on this almost vertical terrain. We were told that a Japanese lady once fell and died and that the guide who had been leading her group was so upset that he went back to try to commit suicide.

Much has been written about the ingenuity of the Incas in using land for agriculture. They developed thousands of strains of potatoes and corn and many other crops. They may have even produced colored cotton. After the Spanish conquest, the potato was exported to the rest of the world and, by increasing the supply of food, saved many places from famines and enabled the expansion of the European population. When potatoes failed in Ireland in the nineteenth century, there was mass starvation and mass migration to the United States. Therefore, the potato indirectly contributed to the Irish immigration to the United States that gave President Kennedy. The Incas experimented a lot with potatoes and corn, generating many varieties of these crops. The diversity of microclimates within short distances due to different altitudes made this possible. Still the locations that were at times used to produce the crops, in the most inaccessible and difficult places, can only indicate that these areas must have become overpopulated. Population pressure must have forced the Incas to exploit any possible piece of available land, especially since the population of the area was much greater before the arrival of the Spanish conquerors.

Machu Picchu remained unknown or better, ignored until 1911 when Hiram Bingham, an archeologist from Yale, "discovered" it. Apparently the city is not even visible from the air because the high mountains block its view for the pilots. Of course the indigenous populations that lived in the area knew about it and were using parts of it for agricultural production. Spanish documents show no evidence of knowledge of this city, and the Incas did not have writing. Machu Picchu was abandoned before the arrival of the Spanish, but the reason remains unknown. The function of Machu Picchu is also a mystery. It was not a normal city, and it makes no sense to think of it as a military fortress. The most plausible explanation is that it was a religious site and a kind of astronomical observatory that allowed religious leaders to determine the days that were more propitious for planting various crops. Some of its temples suggest this function. At a time when there were no calendars, it must have been difficult to guess precisely when to plant crops, and mistakes in the timing could have had serious consequences.

We spent two days visiting most corners of the "city" and taking hundreds of photos. My son, Vito Luigi, also tried his hand at a video.

We discovered that Machu Picchu gets crowded with visitors from around 10:00 am to 3:00 pm. This coincides with the arrival and departure of the train from and to Cuzco. Before 10 and after 3:00, one has the site to oneself. For this reason it is advantageous to stay at the hotel on top of the mountain, just a few steps from the entrance, rather than in Aguas Caliente.

The first night, there was a huge lightning storm. In Machu Picchu the rainy season is generally from November to April. At one point during the raging storm, we were waiting for dinner in the hotel dining room, and the electricity went off. The darkness between each strike of lightning gave us an eerie feeling. Fortunately, the lights came back after a few minutes, and dinner was served. Because of the intense rain, the roof was leaking in various places and buckets had been placed to collect the water. I could not help but think about the bus ride downhill on a muddy slope the next day!

The weather can change very suddenly, and the next morning we woke up very early to a sunny day. Around 7:00 a.m. we went back to the ruins with the idea of going to a place, high on one of the mountains, called "Puente Incaico," or Inca Bridge. From this high point one can enjoy still another view of Machu Picchu. The Puente Incaico is at the end or the beginning of the "Caminos del Inka," the Inca Trail or "Qhapag Non" in the original Inca language. This is a four to five days trail over tall mountains and through deep valleys. After a while, we abandoned our hike. I was afraid to walk on a wet and slippery path, which was no more than two feet wide, at the edge of a deep abyss.

The Inca Trail was part of an extensive communication pathway that the Incas had created before the arrival of the Spaniards. It can be considered one of the first and most successful examples of a cross-border or transnational infrastructure in South America because it connected areas that are now part of Peru, Bolivia, Ecuador, Colombia, Chile and Argentina. It had been created to unify the dispersed territories of the Incan Empire. These roads or, more precisely, foot paths, extended for some twenty thousand miles. This system was so efficient as to allow seafood to be brought to the people in the highlands. People have described the Inca Trail as a spectacle of harmony and safety. Inca's messengers, *chasquis*, moved on foot at great speed along these trails.

The travelers were believed to be protected by the *apus*, the gods of natural forces. Llamas were used to carry weights up to fifty pounds. There were no horses in the Americas before the arrival of the Europeans and no other large animals capable of carrying heavy weights. Thus, even if wheels had been known, they would not have provided much help.

The Trail is one of the most famous world walks together with Cinque Terre in Italy and some others. We met two groups that had walked the Inca Trail. They had hired two local porters for each member of the group, plus two cooks and a guide. They raved about the trip, though they found it very demanding, both physically and emotionally. They told us that one of the guys in the group had wanted to be airlifted within the first two days because he was terrified by the heights in some of the trails. However, he had no choice but to persist. When he completed the hike, he said that he felt like a hero and had been partly liberated of his fears. The group described the pristine environment along the trail and the shock of seeing people again at the end of the journey. They had to go over paths as high as fourteen thousand feet, where they were above or in the middle of the clouds. They often used religious terms to describe the experience, which seems to be a common characteristic of Machu Picchu. As I mentioned earlier, Shirley MacLaine described her spiritual "conversion" after her visit. There are some stones in Machu Picchu that are believed to give energy to those who touch them. My son and I obviously touched them, and I must say that I had more energy when I came back to Washington to my work. But then, this is what normally happens after a short vacation.

The return to Cuzco turned out to be an adventure. On the way down, the steep mountain road was still wet. The bus just missed running into another bus that was carrying, at a rather high speed, some school children up the mountain. The two buses came to a sudden stop at a sharp curve, inches from each other. The driver of the upcoming bus insisted that our bus should maneuver so that his bus could get through. Our bus insisted that the other should make the maneuvers. All this was happening on a narrow wet road cut into a steep mountainside and without guard rails! Eventually, the other bus backed down a little so that our bus could just squeeze through.

The wheel of our bus must have been less than a foot from the edge of the road. I could see the train about one thousand feet almost straight down!

Finally, we made it down the mountain and into the train. I concluded that I must have a strong heart not to have had a heart attack yet. The train left on time. On the way back to Cuzco the train moved counter to the current of the river so that one could assess the steepness of the rail by the speed of the river's water. After a while, the train began to stop every few miles. Each time it stopped someone would step down from the train carrying a container for water. He would go to the river, fill the container, and then go back to the train and throw the water on the train's engine. Apparently it was overheating! The stops became more and more frequent and it appeared that the train did not have the power to go up the hill to Cuzco. When we came to a small train station in the middle of nowhere, the train stopped. The train conductor apparently decided that we could not go forward. We were stopped there for a couple of hours, during which some local women came out of nowhere to sell blankets. For fear of spending the cold night in the train, many passengers decided to buy them, and it must have been a good business day for the local women. To reduce the pressure on the train's engine, the conductor decided to discharge the two rear train cars and transfer the passengers who had been in them to the rest of the train, making it very crowded. With this lighter weight to carry, the train eventually took off and did not have further difficulties. However, a four-hour ride had become a seven-hour ride.

I had made arrangements with the lady from SUNAT to visit a woman in Cuzco, who I had been told had some old colonial keys that might have enriched my collection but it was too late. I much regretted this missed opportunity to add to my key collection. By the way, there is no evidence that the Incas used keys. There must not have been thieves among them. In the evening my son and I had dinner at the hotel in Cuzco, surrounded by a large, noisy and obviously rich group of Colombians. I could not help wonder where their money came from! This was the time when the drug czars of Colombia were all over the news. This was not long before Pablo Escobar, who had become one of the richest men in the world, had been killed. Mark

Bouden gives an interesting account of this in his book, *Killing Pablo: The Hunt for the World's Greatest Outlaw*. The next morning my son and I flew back to Lima, where I was to give a lecture at SUNAT, the national tax administration.

CHAPTER 8

PERU: FROM FUJIMORI BACK TO ALAN GARCÍA

On September 6, 1997, I went back to Peru to speak at the Eighth International Conference Against Corruption. The first such conference had taken place in Washington in 1983 and the seventh had been in Beijing in 1995. By 1997 the world had awakened to the problem of corruption so that the conference in Lima attracted eleven hundred participants from ninety countries. The participants included ministers and famous judges, such as the Italian Judge Gherardo Colombo of Mani Pulite or Tangentopoli fame. It took place in a new hotel, Oro Verde, located near the Japanese embassy. A few months earlier, that embassy had been occupied by the Tupac Amaru. This was a terrorist organization less violent than the Sendero Luminoso. This organization took its name from Tupac Amaru, who opposed the Spanish conquerors and was executed by them in 1572. After his execution, organized opposition to the Spanish conquest finally stopped. The people who had been at the embassy for a party when the takeover occurred were detained by the terrorists for several months to the great embarrassment of the Peruvian government. It was not until a bloody rescue operation, that resulted in the killing of all the terrorists, that they were freed. Fujimori's popularity had soared as the result of this rescue operation.

The niece of the then Minister of Finance, who was working in my department at the IMF in Washington, had told me before I left

Washington about rumors that the terrorists (the Tupac Amaru or even the bloodier Sendero Luminoso) would attempt to disrupt the Corruption Conference by staging a spectacular terrorist incident. For this reason, there was some tension and a lot of security, including guards at each floor of the hotel where the conference was taking place and where I was staying and many soldiers in the area around the hotel.

The opening ceremony on September 7 included speeches by President Fujimori and César Gaviria, then the Secretary General of OAS, among other major political personalities. There was a lot of pomp at the conference's opening, which took place in the auditorium of Santa Ursula School in front of the hotel. All the speakers declared that corruption was a big problem and that it must be stamped out otherwise it would damage democracy and economic development. Gaviria elaborated on the OAS Declaration in which members had stated their firm determination to fight corruption. I always had my doubts as to the value of these political declarations because they were often not followed by concrete actions.

During the opening ceremony, I learned a nice Incan motto: *Ama sua, ama llulla, ama quella*, meaning "Don't be a thief, don't be a liar, don't be lazy." It could be a good guide to policymakers as well as to citizens. This implied that in spite of the lack of keys there must have been thieves among the Incas. A gala concert at the Municipal Theater in the center of Lima and a welcome cocktail, given by the Mayor of Lima, at the Municipal Palace in Plaza Mayor, were planned for the evening. Buses would take the participants from the hotel to the theater and then to the Municipal Palace.

I got into the double-decker bus with two of my Washington colleagues, who were visiting Lima at that time to provide technical assistance on budgeting. When the bus left, I was a bit nervous remembering the rumor I had heard concerning terrorist threats. It struck me that a bus that went through small streets in a large and crowded city was pretty much a sitting duck. We had been on the way for about ten minutes when we heard loud sounds, which could be explosions or the firing of guns. The bus came to a sudden stop, and I was sure that something bad was happening. I could not tell whether it was someone firing at the bus or a bomb exploding nearby. I yelled to my colleagues to duck. However, we soon realized that what had happened was much less menacing. What had really happened was that the plastic covers of the openings on the roof of the bus had hit the ceiling of a low bridge and had fractured into many small pieces making loud noises that sounded like explosions. We were covered with small pieces of plastics that fortunately did not hurt any of the passengers.

Somewhat shaken after the interruption, we proceeded to the Teatro Nacional, an ornate theater with four levels where we heard the Orquestra Sinfonica Nacional of Peru play Mozart, Brahms, and Beethoven. They also played several unknown, and I presumed Peruvian, composers, which I particularly enjoyed because of the novelty of the music. I wondered about many such composers who may have been quite good but who somehow did not become popular. Fashion definitely plays a role in determining the music that we hear. There is no process that systematically revalues past music. For example, I recall that some fifty years ago Scarlatti was as popular as Vivaldi. Today, Vivaldi is far more popular and Scarlatti's music is rarely heard. I was also reminded about a composer from my small town in Italy whose music continues to be played in my town and, as far as I am aware, nowhere else. For a Southern Italian, he has the unlikely name of Nicolo van Westerhout. Each time I hear his music, when I go to my town, I think that it is as good as some of the compositions I hear in concerts. I could not help but think about the process of selection that makes some artists popular while it leaves others in obscurity. The same process works in other fields such as economics and literature. Some economists become very famous during their lifetime, but their name disappears afterwards. How efficient is that process? What role does the nationality of the artist, the language used in the works, his/her ability at self-promotion, fashion, or even chance, play? In the case of Peru, the indigenous people had played their music for thousands of years with original native instruments such as the *laka*, the *loyo*, the *zampoña*, the *queña*, the *bombo*, the *patuto*, and the rainstick. These were predominantly wind and percussion instruments. However, the music could not be written down so that it could only be transmitted though memory. Much of it probably vanished when the Spanish arrived. During colonial times, a few significant composers had left written music but they were probably of European background. Among these, Juan de Araujo (1646-1712) and Tomás de Torrejón y Velasco (1644-1728) are worth noting. The latter wrote the first opera in the Americas called "La Púrpura de la Rosa." There were also some important composers during the Republican period in both Peru and the rest of South America.

At the Municipalidad de Lima we were served *pisco sours* and other cocktails while we admired the magnificent Municipal Palace and the Plaza Mayor, with its majestic cathedral housing Pizarro's remains. The whole complex has been classified of interest to humanity by UNESCO. The Plaza Mayor used to be called Plaza de las Armas before a Mayor of Lima changed the name.

On the morning of September 8, I participated in the conference. James Wolfensohn, then the President of the World Bank, gave a well-articulated and forceful speech from Washington via teleconference. Alfonso Valdivieso, former Attorney General of Colombia, spoke at some length about the connection between drug money and the corruption of government officials and institutions. This problem would in later years move from Colombia to Mexico and create growing problems for the United States. This man had put his life on the line in his attempt to stamp out the influence of drug money in Colombia. He was going to be a presidential candidate at the next election, if he survived. I was reminded of two Colombians that I had known and that had suffered the consequences of having held high official positions. Enrique Low Murtra, an economist who had been Minister of Justice, had been killed by drug smugglers. Rudolf Hommes had been Minister of Finance and had been injured in a shooting.

I particularly enjoyed the talk by Judge John T. Noonan, Jr. of the US, the author of a long and fascinating book on corruption called *Bribes*. Judge Noonan gave an historical account of the use of bribes and mentioned that in ancient Mesopotamia the concept did not even exist. Those visiting important men were expected to bring gifts, just as they were during the Brezhnev era in Soviet Russia. One could not visit a powerful public official empty-handed. In Egypt, one had to take gifts even to the gate of death to get a better reception in the afterworld.

It was not until Roman times when the idea arose that judges and other public officials should not be influenced by gifts. Roman law introduced the concept that both the bribed and the briber are doing something wrong when they accepted or gave bribes. The Romans introduced the novel idea that there are some things that cannot and should not be bought. One should receive freely and should give freely these things. Justice is one of the things that should not be for sale.

In Dante's times, bribery was considered a very serious sin, and the sinners were sent to a deep circle in Hell. Thus, from the time of Mesopotamia to that of Dante, a lot had changed in the way society thought of bribery. Of course, there was far less mutation in actual behavior. Seventeenth century England had zero tolerance for corruption. The US constitution, which must have been influenced by this thinking, explicitly mentions bribery as one of two crimes that would lead to the impeachment of a president, the other being treason. Judge Noonan concluded that corruption and bribery can be stamped out. I had my doubts about this conclusion, although I did believe that instances of bribery can be reduced with good policies and with appropriate penalties. A few years later, while visiting a second-hand bookstore in Bethesda, Maryland, a habit I enjoy, I was able to find a copy of Noonan's large book. I bought it and planned to read it in its entirety someday.

I shared a plenary session panel with Shang Jin Wei, a Chinese economist then teaching at Harvard; James W. Sharer, Secretary General of the World Customs Organization; Baroness Lynda Chalker of Wallasey of the United Kingdom; and Mark Pieth of Switzerland. Professor Wei talked about the impact of corruption on foreign investment and presented some empirical evidence implying that corruption reduces the propensity of foreigners to invest in a given country. Mr. Shaver talked about customs reforms aimed at reducing corruption. The baroness talked about the role that external donors could play in reducing corruption. In her view, these donors should make greater efforts to ensure that foreign aid did not simply transfer money from the taxpayers of donor countries to the Swiss bank accounts of the political leaders in receiving countries.

Some studies, one authored by Professor Alberto Alesina of Harvard and Beatrice Weder, a Swiss economist, had shown that foreign aid often went hand in hand with increased corruption. Professor Pieth discussed the OECD's role in making bribery a punishable offense and in rendering bribes to foreign officials non-deductible for tax purposes. This would level the playing field for countries. At that time, an American company that bribed a foreign official could not deduct the bribe from its taxable income, and the individuals involved could be prosecuted for authorizing the payment. On the other hand, a German company that did the same thing could take a deduction against German taxes with impunity. At a reception at the Moroccan embassy in Washington a few weeks later, former Governor Sununu, who had been chief of staff in the White House, told me that American companies believed that they were losing tens of billions of foreign contracts because of their inability to pay bribes to foreign officials who expected them. American policymakers frequently made this claim during the Clinton Administration, a claim often repeated by Secretary of Commerce Mickey Kantor.

In my speech, I discussed corruption in relation to taxation and to public expenditure. I distinguished grand or political corruption from bureaucratic or administrative corruption. I argued that, in the tax area, two areas to watch in particular were tax incentives and customs, while public investments and procurements were areas to watch in spending. Frequent contacts between officials and private individuals were also major ingredients for corruption. My paper was well received and at the end of my presentation I was interviewed by several journalists. Judge Noonan came to congratulate me on it. The next day, several newspapers reported stories about my intervention. I should add that, after much hesitation and internal discussion, the IMF had begun to take corruption seriously and the Managing Director, Michel Camdessus, became a forceful critic of corrupt practices. The Fund went so far as to suspend negotiations for Fund-supported programs with several countries on the basis of corruption issues. The Pope was scheduled to send a message to the conference but, for technical reasons, the message did not come. Thus, the Conference missed having his Sanctity's blessing.

After the conference, I went looking for old keys to buy for my collection. I bought a couple of old ones, perhaps as old as colonial times, which for Peru meant before 1824. I also went to see a magnificent exhibition of paintings by Osualdo Guayasamin, at the Museo de la Nacion. I remain impressed by this Ecuadorian painter who died ten years ago. Perhaps, he had been the most famous Latin American painter in the 1950s and 1960s, but his fame seems to have declined somewhat in more recent years. Some of his paintings have extraordinary power and would look well even next to some of Picasso's paintings. In fact, they immediately remind one of Picasso's work. Why is Guayasamin not more famous? One reason is that he was very much a leftist. One of the books I have on him, published in Spain, shows photos of the artist with Mao Tse Tung, Ho Chi Min, Krushchev, Salvador Allende, Fidel Castro, and other famous leftist personalities. There could thus be no confusion about Guayasamin's political leanings.

In a long write-up on Guayasamin in the late 1950s, when his fame was on the rise, *Time Magazine* praised his extraordinary talent but predicted that he would pay a price because of his leftist bias and the rage that comes out of his paintings. In the mid-1960s, while I was visiting Quito, I had the privilege to spend a few hours with him at his house and used some of my savings to buy one of his paintings. I had the option to buy the remaining two that comprised the triptych, *Triptico de los Desesperados*. I did not take him up on this offer and I always regretted not having done so. I was somewhat amused at the time to notice that the check I had given him to pay for the painting was deposited in Switzerland. I suppose that even leftist painters must protect their assets against bad government policies. In Quito, Ecuador, there are two splendid Guayasamin Museums containing collections of his works. Because of Guayasamin's advocacy, Ecuador passed a law requiring that large buildings spend three percent of the building cost on art works. Given my bias, I find this kind of regulation attractive. Similar laws now exist in some other countries.

For the last night in Lima, the conference organizers staged a "Noche Peruana" at the Museo de la Nacion. I was expecting something typically Peruvian, such as an Incan show, but instead an Afro-Brazilian style singer named Eva Ayllon was the performer. She is considered the diva of Afro-Peruvian music, which is very popular in Peru. She is a terrific singer and entertainer but, my opinion was that she might have been more appropriate in Salvador de Bahia, Brazil, than in Lima.

Later I was told that there were four hundred thousand blacks in Peru and that Afro culture had been having a large impact on the country. So, perhaps, she was not as out of place as I thought.

I must report on two sad developments after my departure from Peru. The first is that, in spite of all the rhetoric against corruption at the conference, evidence of the Fujimori administration's corruption came to light a short time after the conference. Fujimori had to escape from Peru and take refuge in Japan. His main adviser, Colonel Vladimiro Montesinos, was captured on video buying the votes of members of parliament. This was an extraordinary end for a shy agricultural economist who, as the result of a protest vote, had found himself to be the President of Peru. There was speculation that Fujimori was actually born in Japan, where he took refuge after his disgrace. If these reports were correct, he could not legally have become president of Peru because, according to the constitution, a president must be born in Peru. The Peruvian government tried to bring him back to Peru for his trial. At the end of 2005, Fujimori attempted to return to Peru by way of Chile where he was stopped and arrested. For a while Chile refused to extradite him to Peru. He was eventually extradited and tried for various alleged crimes. He is now in a Peruvian jail. In Peru he has still a substantial political following, including a daughter and a brother in parliament. It is sad to realize how many Latin American leaders have been affected by the disease of corruption over the years.

From time to time I have used the example of Fujimori becoming president of Peru as a good example of globalization. At the time of Christopher Columbus or Ferdinand Magellan, who could have thought that a Japanese man would become president of the country that had been at the heart of the Incan Empire? The corrupting role of Colonel Montesinos on the Fujimori's administration received a lot of attention. Some believe that Montesinos had blackmailed Fujimori, forcing him to go along with his acts of corruption. During his career as a corruptor, Montesinos infiltrated various institutions, including SUNAT. His technique had been to create parallel administrative positions, such as an associate director, within the administrations so that appointees could handle his corrupt dealings while the structure of the institution appeared unchanged. This model of corruption deserves to be studied because it is likely to be used elsewhere.

The other sad development was more personal. After the conference I returned to Washington and left behind the two colleagues who were helping the Peruvian government to reform its budgetary system. One of the colleagues, Lazlo Garamfalvi, had been the one sitting next to me on the bus when I thought that we were being attacked by terrorists. I learned that the morning after I left he had had a heart attack and had died in his hotel room. This was very shocking and sad news for me and, of course, for his family and colleagues at the Fund.

In August 1998, I went back to Lima for a short visit to give the "Carlos Diaz Alejandro Lecture" at the XVI Latin American Meeting of the Econometric Society. The lecture was named after the late Carlos Diaz Alejandro who had been a prominent Cuban development economist. He had taught at Yale and Columbia Universities. He had been a specialist on Latin American economies and especially on their economic histories. I had met him in the 1960s at the *Alliance for Progress* in Washington where he had been doing some consulting. Many economists interested in Latin American developments attended the Econometric Society meeting. The title of my lecture was "Corruption, Trade and Development," a topic on which I had written some related papers. I do not have specific recollections worth reporting from this meeting except that I became aware of the growth of private universities in Latin America. These private institutions had slowly started filling the gap left by politicized and decaying public ones. The meeting was held at one of these private universities.

I went back to Lima on July 12, 2004 at the invitation of the Peruvian government. By this time I had retired from the IMF and, after spending a couple years in the Italian government, I was working as a consultant for the Inter-American Development Bank in Washington. The visit lasted only three days, consisting of several meetings and seminars. Jaime Pinto, then the Peruvian representative at the IDB, accompanied me. In preparation for the trip, I did some reading and some catching up on what had been happening in Peru, especially on the economic scene, since my last visit in August 1998.

1997 had been the last good year for the Fujimori administration. After that, the period of economic recovery that began in 1991 had come to an end. This period had seen an end to hyperinflation, a recovery in tax revenue and in the real gross domestic product, a sharp fall in external debt, and the enactment of various economic reforms, including the privatization of several public enterprises. It ended partly because of the financial crises that hit various countries throughout the world, but especially because of political developments in Peru.

Between 1997 and 2001, Peru was shrouded in an overall atmosphere of crisis. Fujimori had decided to run for reelection, in defiance of the Constitutional provision that limited a president to one term. Corruption had spread in part because Colonel Montesinos had tried to buy votes in congress to support Fujimori's bid. Between 1998 and 2001, growth had slowed down and reforms had stalled. After its peak in 1997, tax revenue fell until 2002, when it started rising again under the Alejandro Toledo administration. The period after 2001 has been much better in terms of macroeconomic developments. For the past decade the rate of growth of Peru has exceeded five percent per year, which is very good by Latin American standards. In macroeconomic terms the Peruvian economy was the top performer in Latin America during this period. In 2008, the rating agencies gave Peru investment status so that it was again able to borrow from the international financial market. Its inflation rate has also been very low.

During my visit in 2004, the SUNAT supervisors gave me a document and made power-point presentations indicating that significant progress had been achieved in the past three years. The tax burden had gone up, reaching thirteen percent of GDP in 2004, not including social security taxes. This was close to the record reached in 1997 before taxes started falling. With social security taxes, the tax burden would be about sixteen percent of GDP, still below but not far from the Latin American average. The activities of the tax administration had been integrated with those of the customs administration, allowing a useful exchange of information between the two administrations. There had been various administrative improvements that allowed increases in income and sales taxes. There were some issues, however, that remained in discussion.

The first was what to do with the two hundred or so tax incentives that reduced tax revenue, distorted the allocation of resources, and complicated tax administration. It seems that some things never change, for this was the same problem that I had found in my first visit to Peru in the late 1960s. Some of these tax incentives had perverse effects. For example, the incentive not to tax gasoline or diesel used in the Selva or the Sierra presumably to stimulate agricultural production had become a major subsidy for the producers of illegal drugs who were the major consumers of gasoline and diesel in those areas. Products reportedly produced in the Sierra and the Selva and thus benefiting from the tax incentives were often produced in Lima. What traveled were not the products but the invoices. As is often the case, tax incentives had produced powerful lobbies, including that of the producers of illegal drugs. This made it difficult for the government to remove them.

The second issue was that of the income tax. This tax was considered high by Peruvian entrepreneurs and investors, even though the rates were very low and it hardly produced any revenue. I attended a public meeting that included important personalities such as Pedro Pablo Kuchinsky, then the Minister of Finance and the Prime Minister, and the Director of SUNAT. Using data that SUNAT had provided me, I pointed out that, in a country of some twenty-eight million people, only about one percent of the population paid *any* income tax. Of these, only one in every seventy taxpayers (3,877 individuals in all) was subjected to the modest marginal rate of thirty percent. Of course the average rate was much lower. These 3,877 individuals represented about one in every 7,000 Peruvians. 263,000 were subjected to a marginal tax rate of only fifteen percent. Furthermore, dividends and interest incomes were tax exempt. In spite of these statistics, some people still argued that these income taxes were contributing to the informal activities that prevailed in the Peruvian economy, or that they were negatively affecting the growth of the official economy. In an interview in a popular television program, the interviewer actually pressed me to state that high taxes were damaging the Peruvian economy. He was taken aback when I challenged that conclusion with data that I had available.

The third issue, and one that had also become a hot one in Chile, Peru, and Bolivia, was how to tax foreign companies that exploited mineral resources. This issue had become very topical due to the sharp rise in commodity prices and the fact that mineral resources were often in the hands of foreign companies. Should these companies be taxed only on their net profits or also on their production through royalties? The problem with taxing profits alone is that these companies often show no profits for many years. This is either because of the occasional low prices of the extracted minerals, or because of account manipulation. I lacked specific knowledge in this area so I did not take a firm position. However, I ventured to state that royalties could be justified for two reasons: the environmental degradation that often accompanies these mining activities, and the fact that these companies, by extracting minerals from the Peruvian soil, would leave the country with less potential resources for the future, and thus poorer. At the time of my visit a story in *The Economist* had mentioned that an American company, which for over twenty-five years had always reported losses from a copper mining activity in Chile, had sold the Chilean activity for US$1.3 billion. One wonders why one would pay this money for an enterprise that has always lost money. I refrained, however, from taking a position on the size of the royalty.

The fourth issue had to do with the developing political pressures for fiscal decentralization. In the past, I had cautioned against this road, which called for shifting more spending responsibility to sub-national or local governments. I had argued that fiscal decentralization and especially fiscal federalism, in which political power over fiscal decisions is partly shifted to sub-national governments, has often led to macroeconomic difficulties. In Peru, however, I became aware that this trend was likely to gain momentum because of powerful political developments. These developments had appeared most forcefully in Bolivia, but also in other Latin American countries, such as Guatemala, Ecuador, and Mexico. The process of democratization had created strong pressures on the part of ethnically diverse groups (especially indigenous descendants) to have more of a say in the running of their affairs. They were tired of having ethnically different people making decisions for them from far away capitals. In Bolivia, the discovery of natural gas had accentuated these pressures and in 2005 it would lead to the election of Evo Morales, the first Latin American elected President with a fully indigenous background.

The discovery of natural resources in a particular area can also create major political difficulties especially when the area is populated by either ethnically or culturally diverse populations. If the resources are appropriated by the central government, and if the country's income distribution is very uneven, as it is in many Latin American countries, the chance is small that the local populations in those areas will gain much from the exploitation and the exportation of the minerals. History has taught these populations that the benefits from the exploitation of these resources will go to others, such as foreigners or well-placed and rich nationals. It will be hard to believe promises that the revenue will be used for "development." Due to these historical trends, there is increasing pressure to turn some of these areas into independent nations, or at least pressure for fiscal decentralization, which would leave the resources in the hands of regional governments. This has happened in Nigeria, Indonesia, Russia, and Sudan, among other places. In some of these places civil wars have been the outcome of these pressures.

Given the lack of good institutions outside of Lima capable of monitoring resources and of using them efficiently, it is unlikely that fiscal decentralization would be macroeconomically responsible or that it would promote policies that use resources efficiently. However, decentralization is a trend that the Peruvian Government is not likely to be able to stop. I advised officials to proceed slowly and to concentrate on creating satisfactory local public expenditure management systems. This would help ensure that the use of resources is carefully monitored and that the resources used locally go to their intended purposes. Unfortunately, evidence from various countries seems to indicate that corruption may be more prevalent at the local level.

During my stay in Lima there was a general strike, supported by Alan García and his party, Alianza Popular Revolucionaria (APRA). The strike had limited success in part because it coincided with the soccer championship, Copa America. One lesson for those who plan these strikes is that they should not coincide with popular events, especially important soccer games. In Latin America, and perhaps even in Europe, soccer can offer a big competition to politics. At the time of my visit, the popularity of Peru's president, Alejandro Toledo, had reached such a low level that there were bets going on as to when the president's falling approval rating would equal the country's rising GDP growth rate. I joked that if that equality materialized, it would be because the rate of growth would rise and not because the popularity of the president would fall any more.

The low approval rating of President Toledo was surprising in light of the economy's good performance during his administration, at least in terms of macroeconomic developments. Perhaps the reasons were to be found outside these developments, such as in the accusations of corruption involving some members of the president's family. Or perhaps it was the fact that income distribution had remained very uneven so that much of the economic growth was benefiting the few, usual suspects. In any case, the IMF was giving high grades to the Peruvian government for its running of the economy. This praise was justified in terms of the big numbers, that is, in terms of macroeconomic developments. It was less justified in terms of what was happening to perhaps 75 percent of the population.

A surprising development for me at that time was the return to politics and the growing popularity of Alan García. Apparently the economic mess that he was accused of having caused during his administration in the 1980s was not a sufficient reason for keeping him unpopular and out of the running for the next elections. During the election he was once again talking about nationalizing enterprises, closing trade, controlling prices and so on. These were the policies that had contributed to the earlier mess. I realized that the fifteen years since he had ended his term had created a kind of asymmetrical information problem between those who had been adults during that period and thus remembered it, and those who had reached voting age after that. In a country with a fast population growth, fifteen years is a long time and the "median voter" keeps changing at a fast rate. Additionally the very poor income distribution and the high incidence of poverty—54.3 percent of the population were classified as poor, and twenty-four percent were classified as living in extreme poverty in 2002—may imply that populist promises will always have a strong following in these circumstances. The very poor often do not share in the improvements that come from good macroeconomic policies.

This brings me back to the question of the uneven income distribution. There has been much controversy over the years on whether governments should focus on economic growth and forget about equity; or whether they should focus on both economic growth *and* equity. Obviously it is always a mistake to focus exclusively on equity because it often ends up in redistributing poverty rather than wealth. Some economists have argued that governments should not be distracted by the pursuit of equity. In their view a faster rate of growth will eliminate poverty at a faster pace than policies aimed directly at poverty reduction. They point to China and to a lesser extent India, as countries that are rapidly reducing absolute poverty because of their fast growth. Thus, these economists believe that Peru should be happy with its good rate of growth in recent years and promote even higher rates.

I always had some difficulty with this view. While recognizing that growth is essential and fundamental to the alleviation of *absolute* poverty one must recognize various factors. First, in democratic societies with highly uneven income distributions, it may be difficult for governments to pursue pro growth policies that ignore income distribution over the long run. Sooner or later the population will start demanding different and most likely populist policies, thus detracting from the country's growth. When income distribution is very uneven, the poor represent the majority of the population and they will not continue to support policies that in their view benefit mainly the top five or ten percent of the population. The trickle-down theory is not likely to impress them.

Second, the pursuit of growth will at some point require more ethical policies, especially policies that increase the capacity to produce, i.e., the human capital of the poor. Third, and perhaps more importantly, it is a mistake to think of poverty in absolute terms, say less than $1 or $2 a day. Poverty is mostly a relative concept. If the top five percent of the population is doing well because of economic growth, while the bottom fifty percent is doing just a bit better than previously, this cannot be considered a desirable development even though *absolute* poverty may be falling.

For these reasons I felt that, despite Peru's good macroeconomic performance during the Toledo administration, the one that had succeeded the Fujimori administration, as long as the income distribution remained so uneven, Alan García's comeback should not be ruled out as a possibility. I was thus not particularly surprised when he won the election. Actually, the fact that García's main opponent promoted far more leftist policies probably made him look more conservative and helped his campaign. Perhaps, it may be worthwhile to mention that for the period between 1991 and 2000 surveys about perceptions of past progress and future prospects indicated that a surprisingly large proportion of respondents did not acknowledge progress over that period. Thus perceptions may diverge from the message that one gets from macroeconomic developments. This raises the question of whether the data or the perceptions are conveying a more accurate picture of reality. Perceptions may be wrong but data may lie.

In spite of my busy schedule, I managed to indulge for a couple hours in an important cultural activity. I visited a private collection, referred to as the Museo Enrico Poli, that I had been told which it was definitely a must-see. To visit this museum one needs to make a specific appointment. My visit had been arranged by the Tax Administration. Enrico Poli is an Italian- born individual who had gone to Peru in 1945, immediately at the end of World War Two. I was told that he had never returned to Italy even for a visit. He owned a hotel in Lima and developed an interest in, or better yet an obsession with, collecting rare objects from the pre-Columbian period and the colonial period. These objects included paintings, pieces of furniture, items in silver or even gold, and many items made of terracotta, the famous *huacos*. He must have developed good contacts with tomb raiders, the so-called *huaqueros*. The "museum" is in his house in a good area of Lima. It would be a big understatement to say this collection is extraordinary. It is unlikely there are many other places where so much outstanding artwork has been crammed in so little space. And all has been done in a remarkably tasteful way. During the visit, my wife and I were the only guests on this tour. The tour was guided by Poli's son who was also named Enrico. He explained in detail the many outstanding pieces contained in the museum. I bought a beautiful catalogue of the collection.

After my visit to the museum, the President of the Central Bank offered a luncheon there. During the lunch we discussed what would happen to this remarkable collection when the aging Enrico Poli passed away. The concern was that his heirs would begin to sell parts of it so that this carefully assembled collection would become dispersed. I volunteered the view that the Central Bank could make a gift to Peru by buying the collection and making it a public museum.

In early February 2008, coming back from a trip to Chile, my wife and I decided to stop in Peru for about a week to visit Lima, Cuzco and Machu Picchu. This was a purely private, tourist visit. I was particularly interested in spending some time in Cuzco because I had not been able to do so in my earlier visits. By this time I had become very interested in the Latin American churches built by the Spanish and the Portuguese in the sixteenth and seventeenth centuries. We flew to Lima and stayed at a modern hotel in the area of San Isidro. The hotel was in the middle of large grove of olive trees, which had been planted by the Spanish. These trees, combined with the fact that the area is predominantly peopled by Europeans, some of whom came to Peru after World War Two, gives one the impression of being in Europe.

At the hotel we enjoyed that most Peruvian delicacy that is *ceviche*. We accompanied it with another Peruvian tradition, the *pisco sour*. Ceviche is raw fish marinated with lemon juice. It thus reminds one of sushi, although the taste is quite different. The origin of the word *ceviche* is uncertain. It may have come from an Arab word or from the reaction of the first American who ate it and exclaimed "son of a bitch!" While *pisco* is a most Peruvian drink and institution, it turns out, to the annoyance of the Peruvians, that Chile is producing far more *pisco* than Peru. Adding insult to injury, Chile is also calling its product *pisco*. This would be like calling a sparkling wine produced in the state of New York *champagne*. The question of Chile's right to call its product *pisco* has created a cold war between the two countries that is almost as hot as the Pacific War of 1879-83 among Chile and Peru and Bolivia. For a humorous discussion of this hot diplomatic issue between the two countries one should look at Daniel Titinger's *Dios es Peruano*.

Lima was founded by Francisco Pizarro in 1535, replacing Cuzco as the capital of the Spanish Empire in the New World. It was established in what is essentially a desert area. This remarkable city developed with a mixture of architectural styles and races. The mixing of races (original inhabitants, Spanish, other Europeans, Chinese, Japanese, Africans and others) has formed a race of *mestizo* that characterizes a large share of the population.

Some important sites include: Parque de la Esposicion, Columbus Avenue, Palacio de Justicia, and especially Plaza San Martin, with the Presidential Palace, the Cathedral, the nearby Hotel Bolivar, and the

Teatro Colon. During the years of terrorism and economic stagnation from the 1970s to the early 1990s, the center of Lima declined because of the economy and the rising crime rate. The financial offices moved to Miraflores and San Isidro, and the Hotel Bolivar, one of the grand old hotels of Latin America, closed down. Many buildings were abandoned. In an interesting twist, during the Fujimori administration, yellow became his preferred color. He had the new schools and the new public buildings painted yellow to advertise his concern for economic and social development. At that time the Venezuelan embassy in the center of Lima was also painted yellow. In 2008, when Fujimori was in a Peruvian jail awaiting sentencing and Hugo Chavez was in power in Venezuela, the Venezuelan embassy changed its color to red, perhaps to better reflect the current Venezuelan policies.

A remarkable site in Lima is the Complex of San Francisco, with the Church of San Francisco, the Santuario, and the Monasterio. Much of the complex is made of wood because of the earthquakes that have occasionally destroyed it. It is an extremely rich complex with beautiful paintings and carvings and with and an extraordinary Christ carved in ivory that was imported from the Philippines. Some of the walls have frescoes, but these have for the most part been covered by paintings and by beautiful tiles made by local *mestizo* artists. Under the monastery are catacombs where monks, priests, and others were buried in the past. It is estimated that the ossuary contains no less than twenty-five thousand skeletons. The catacombs reminded me of the bizarre and macabre Cemetery of the Capuchins in Rome, a few steps from Piazza Barberini. That cemetery is also in the basement of a church. The bizarre part is that in Rome the thousands of human bones and skulls have been arranged in beautiful floral patterns. The sign at the entrance reminds one that "you are what we were; we are what you will be." This is clearly an accurate statement and provides a perfect forecast. However, I doubt that many of the visitors would look forward to the time when their remains could become part of a floral arrangement. It should also be noted that the Order of St. Francis must have played a major role in the New World in the sixteenth and seventeenth centuries. This is evident in the many beautiful churches dedicated to the founding saint in countries such as Peru, Ecuador, and Brazil.

The Plaza San Martin is a very charming plaza that bustles with life during the day. It is one of the "living rooms" of the town and a good example of the many beautiful plazas that one finds in Latin American and European countries. I remain puzzled as to why North American cities generally do not have plazas. There are no really famous plazas in American cities such as one finds in European cities like Rome, Paris, Brussels, Madrid, and Moscow, or in Latin American countries like Mexico, Peru, and Argentina. Historically, these plazas were where important events took place. American cities have squares and circles but not true plazas. The difference is not just a question of terminology. Somehow the European concept of a plaza, that is a place surrounded by beautiful and often official buildings, where citizens go to walk or to just sit around, does not seem to be part of the American culture.

In Plaza San Martin, one popular tourist attraction was an old man with his dog. The old man was modestly dressed, but the dog was elegantly fitted with a neat coat, a nice hat, and fashionable sunglasses that could have been designed by Prada. The dog was a sight that could not be missed because it seemed dressed for a major ceremony. Tourists would take photos of themselves with the dog, after making some small payment to the dog's owner, of course. The dog was the man's capital and provided him with a good rate of return. This made me think of the many ingenious ways in which people make a living. It also made me think about the informal sector in Latin America that is reported to account for large shares of employment, sometimes exceeding fifty percent. Many of the people in the informal sector use their imagination to make a living, as the old man with the dog was doing.

I was reminded of another old man in Teguichigalpa, Honduras who would walk in the main street carrying a large pot made of clay under his arm. His ruse was to pretend to collide with an innocent visitor, preferably a foreigner. The collision would result in the pot falling to the ground and breaking. This "accident" would be followed by some crying on the part of the old man. He would lament the damage suffered. The visitor would have little alternative but to pull his wallet and make a payment for the broken pot, a payment that would far exceed the cost of the pot. Economists would probably approve of the activity of the man with the dog, which may have been producing some real value with such as entertainment for the people. However, they would not approve of the less honest activity of the man with the pot. In the terminology of economists, the first activity would be considered Pareto improving. The second would not. But both would provide a living to those practicing them.

After our brief visit to Lima, we flew to Cuzco. We spent the night there and drank the coca that helped us to become acclimatized to the high altitude. The next morning, we took the train to Aguas Caliente, the little village at the foot of Machu Picchu. This was my second visit to Machu Picchu in thirteen years. The train had become more modern than it was on my earlier visit in 1995. Lunch was served and there was even a little fashion show followed by the sale of some clothing items by the railroad company. However, the tracks had not changed and it still took about four hours to go the seventy miles to Aguas Caliente. When we arrived in Aguas Caliente, there was the usual confusion at the railroad station. We were met by a couple of young men from the hotel where we had made reservations for the night. We were disappointed to find out that the hotel was in Aguas Caliente itself and not in Machu Picchu. We gave them our luggage and immediately joined the tour for Machu Picchu.

A man named Hector led the group. He was not as good a guide as I had hoped and he told us some stories that were of doubtful accuracy. The climb to Machu Picchu is now restricted to official buses so that it has probably become safer. Also, some vegetation has been planted on the side of the road that looks down to the railroad station. The bushes do not provide any protection to the buses but, by providing some screening, they help remove some of the fear that one had earlier. The road seemed to be better paved than the time before. We climbed the 1500 feet to the top and spent the next three hours hiking, taking photos, and occasionally listening to Hector. We visited the temple of the sun, the temple of the condor, and the ceremonial and astronomical areas where one can see the famous magic stone. The stone has been cordoned off so that it can no longer be touched. We were lucky that the sun came out for a while but toward the end of the tour it started raining. We took a lot of photos and enjoyed the visit. However, I concluded that the second visit to a place is never as exciting as the first visit because the excitement of discovery is gone. One knows what one will find. It is also worth mentioning that the small hotel, next to the entrance of Machu Picchu, where I had stayed the first time, had built a large cafeteria for tourists. Machu Picchu, although clearly still extraordinary, had become less mysterious and more for tourists over the last thirteen years.

We rode the bus down the mountain to Aguas Caliente and looked for the Hotel Sumaq, the newly opened hotel where we would spend the night. While looking for the hotel we could concentrate on the surrounding area. The village is located in a very narrow and steep canyon where the mountains come down in almost vertical walls. The canyon is no wider than a couple hundred feet. Hotel Sumaq is built against a vertical wall that is at least a thousand feet tall. I could not help but hope that the mountain was a stable one because any instability could result in land slides or huge rocks falling directly on the hotel.

In front of the hotel, separating it from the opposite wall of the canyon, there is the narrow, two-lane road that leads to Machu Picchu. During that time of year, a most raging and deafening torrent runs immediately next to the road. The torrent moved so fast that it reminded me of a large waterfall that moved horizontally instead of vertically. It was making large waves and creating circular currents. The water level was just a couple feet below that of the road, making the road wet. I again hoped that the rains in the mountains that fed the torrent stayed within the normal range. It would not take much to submerge the canyon with the village of Aguas Caliente and our hotel.

We must have been the first guests at the Hotel Sumaq because they were still putting the finishing touches to the hotel. Our room smelled of fresh paint which made us to want to open the window. However, opening the windows meant being deafened by the roar of the torrent. Thus we had considerable difficulties in sleeping. The next morning we returned to Cuzco by train and to the lovely Hotel Santo Domingo where we had stayed earlier. The return was uneventful and far less exciting than the first time. We spent the next day visiting some of the churches of Cuzco. Cuzco contains many important monuments and churches. The churches were often built on top of former Inca temples, just as the Catholic religion was superimposed on the religions of the Incas. In both cases, one need not dig much to find the previous cultures. The main plazas accommodated the symbols of the main powers, the church, the state, and the authorities of the town. In Cuzco there are several beautiful plazas. The most important plaza is dominated by two imposing churches, the Basilica Cathedral of Cuzco and the Jesuit church of the Compañia de Jesus.

The Basilica Cathedral of Cuzco is a massive, austere and imposing church that has the same visual effect as the cathedral in the Zócalo of Mexico City. Construction of the Basilica started in 1538, following a request by the conquistadors to create a Diocese for the Friar Valverde, the one who had attempted the instantaneous conversion to Catholicism of Atahualpa. Pope Paul III had issued a Papal Bull on January 13th, 1536, creating the Diocese. The church was not completed until 1668 after overcoming many hurdles, such as architectural changes, lack of money, and damages from earthquakes. Some of the stones of the cathedral came from the fortress of Saqsaywaman. It was built on top of two important Incan palaces, the Suntur Wasi and the Kiswan Kancha. The inside is in the shape of a cross with five Naves. The interior of the cathedral is incredibly rich with marvelous artistry by *mestizo* workmen. There are lots of paintings of San Isidro and a remarkable *Last Supper*. San Isidro, the patron saint of agriculture, was indigenized to make him more attractive to the indigenous population. There is a beautiful wood altar with fantastic carvings covered by a silver altar that has simple lines and was added later. There are many side niches which are richly decorated. Particularly remarkable is the Capilla del Santisimo as well as the *Christo Negro*, or Black Christ, a marvelous sculpture made black by the earlier use of candles.

As was often the case in Latin America, a kind of religious competition existed between the Jesuit churches and those built by other religious orders. The Church of the Compañia de Jesus, on the same square where the cathedral is located, was begun in the year 1654 and was completed only seventeen years later, indicating the greater efficiency or power of the Jesuits. It is obvious that the Compañia was built as a challenge to the cathedral. The main altar of the church of the Compañia de Jesus is immense, seventy feet high and forty feet wide. It is made of cider wood covered by gold. It includes naked women, presumably as a sign of fertility. It is a truly outstanding example of the *cusqueño baroque* and of the artistic talent of the craftsmen of Cuzco who made it. The church contains beautiful paintings, some painted by the Italian painter Bernardo Democrito Vici de Camerino, who originated the Cuzco School followed by *mestizo* painters. The Jesuits may have overplayed their hand. In 1767 they were expelled from Cuzco. It is difficult to find more beautiful churches anywhere else. If one is looking for a very good book on the churches of Cuzco, *The Churches of Cuzco: History and Architecture* by Oscar Chara Zerecedo and Viviana Caparó Gil is worth reading.

The next day, my wife and I went on a tour of the Valle Sagrada. It was Carnival time, which made the tour more interesting because many Carnival- related activities were taking place in the streets and even in the countryside. Carnival festivities have become an integral part of the local culture. We saw groups of people moving around wearing masks and dancing. In a town called Pisac we admired dancing competitions among groups of young performers from nearby villages. They were wearing beautiful customs and performing indigenous music and dances. The dances and the customs could have come straight from the times of the Incas. The competition took place on a platform built in the main square and under a light rain. The performance had attracted a lot of spectators.

I learned that the Incas believed in reincarnation and that they believed that the Milky Way was a spiritual bridge connecting Pisac to Machu Picchu. In some areas there were fireworks. We also learned that in the Sacred Valley there are three hundred fifty types of corn. In a coffee shop where we stopped, I took photos of a bowl with many different colored varieties of corn. Speaking of how colorful everything was, we even saw blue-eyed alpacas.

After Pisac, we visited Calca, another town that had a large sign at the entrance: "no se vende, se difiende." "Not for sale but to be defended." In another village, Orientaytango, where there is an important Incan ruin, there were groups of kids, some as large as twenty, going around with buckets of water that they would throw on anyone passing by. We had to close the windows of the bus so as not to be doused. Apparently this is one of the normal activities during Carnival. We finally visited Chinchero, the potato capital of the Incas. I learned that to protect the potatoes from insects they were squeezed and dried out, which made them as hard as stones. In this form they could be stored for a long time. It was a kind of safety net in case of famine.

All in all, I have come to feel that Peru is truly one of the most interesting countries to visit. It is interesting both economically and especially culturally.

CHAPTER 9

CHILE: THE COUNTRY AT THE END OF THE WORLD

My first contact with Chile came in early 1970, when I worked as a consultant for the economics department of the OAS, the regional, political association of American countries. At that time Chile was attracting a lot of attention in Washington because of President Salvador Allende's election and the leftist policies pursued by his government. The economic department of the OAS was preparing a report on the Chilean economy, and asked me to write a chapter on the public finances. A particular concern of this chapter would be the high fiscal deficit and the relationship between the very high rate of inflation, which was seen as the outcome of the government's economic policy, and tax revenue.

The prevailing view among economists was that inflation raises real tax revenue through what economists called the "fiscal drag," a term that had become popular at the time. Inflation pushed people's nominal (money) incomes toward higher income brackets, meaning a higher tax rate in a progressive income tax, thus increasing their tax burden and raising government revenue. The assumption was that the government would benefit from this inflation. However, in Chile this was not happening. At that time the government's real tax revenue (that is, corrected for inflation) was not rising but falling. Taxes were falling as a share of GDP. I started to see the possibility, but only vaguely, that in a period of high inflation, if taxes are paid with delays (from the time that a taxable event occurs) the government will receive money that has been reduced in value by the effect of inflation. The higher the rate of inflation, and the longer the delays in payments, the greater the revenue loss experienced by the government. Thus, under these circumstances it would be the taxpayers that would gain and not the taxpayers. I would later pursue this line of thinking and refine the theory in the context of my work in Argentina in 1976 and 1977, a period when Argentina would also experience a period of very high inflation associated with falling tax revenue. This work resulted in what came to be called the "Tanzi effect" in economic textbooks. It was published in an often cited article in the IMF Staff Papers, the economic review of the IMF, in March 1977. An intuitive description of that effect was reported in Chapter III of my book, *Argentina: An Economic Chronicle*. I did not travel to Chile at that time because the OAS was cutting expenses due to budgetary difficulties. I wrote the chapter in Washington using the information that I had available. In Argentina I could test the theory with actual data.

In the early 1970s there were many Chilean expatriates working for the OAS and for other international organizations in Washington. As had happened with Cubans in the late 1950s when Fidel Castro took over, many Chileans, especially those with higher education, left Chile worried about their and Chile's future. They feared that Chile would go the way of Cuba. Chilean society had become sharply divided between those who were pro-Allende and those who were against Allende and his policies. This division was partly along income and, to some extent, educational, lines. The debates between members of the two groups became sharp and increasingly emotional.

In trying to change Chilean society in a short period of time, and to improve the highly uneven income distribution that characterized and continues to characterize that society, the democratically elected Allende administration started taking some legal shortcuts and bending some existing rules, occasionally even breaking them. For example, petty crimes, such as stealing, came to be seen as the inevitable result of social injustice and not as criminal acts to be punished. The courts started taking a more relaxed attitude towards the perpetrators of these crimes. This infuriated those who opposed Allende and those who were the victims of these crimes. At the time the economy was going through a difficult period with high and rising inflation. There was an increasing fear, on the part of some, that the democratically elected government would take Chile into a non-democratic end. Salvador Allende's friendship with Castro contributed to this fear. There were also sharp debates among Allende sympathizers, between those who wanted to take Chile democratically in a direction similar to that of, say, Sweden, and those who wanted to go the non-democratic Cuban way.

Eventually, a military junta headed by General Augusto Pinochet led a military coup against the Allende government. This coup was reportedly welcomed or even backed by the Nixon administration, particularly by Henry Kissinger. The coup resulted in the suicide of President Allende in the presidential palace, La Moneda. Allende was reported to have used a gun that had been given to him as a gift by Fidel Castro. The coup occurred on the same day as the terrorist attack on the Twin Towers and on the Pentagon, September 11, however twenty-eight years earlier. Thus, September 11 is remembered for different tragic events in both the United State and Chile. Given the sharp division that existed at that time in the Chilean society, the coup was welcomed by many of those who had opposed Allende and was sharply condemned by many inside and outside Chile, especially by Europeans. Many lamented that a democratically elected government had been replaced by a repressive and authoritarian one. In the minds of many Europeans, General Pinochet soon acquired a place right next to the Devil, as the incarnation of evil,

Allende's fall was followed by the persecution of many of his followers, his sympathizers and others who were considered enemies of the new regime. In the period after the coup many people disappeared and were presumably killed by the military. Some were allegedly dropped from helicopters in the Pacific Ocean. The "official" estimate of the number of *desaparecidos* is 3,197, although it is difficult to determine the actual number that was probably higher. Also, thousands were arrested and tortured, many in Villa Grimaldi, a secret detention and torture center in Santiago which is now a memorial to the victims of the Pinochet regime. Some pregnant women who had been, or had been suspected of being, on Allende's side were killed after they gave birth to their babies and the babies were adopted, or better appropriated, by some of the military officers. A Chilean film, *Hijos*, captured some of the tragedies connected with these "adoptions." In some cases the adopted children would grow up and discover, or suspect, that their "parents" were in fact the killers or part of the group responsible for the death of their true parents.

The Pinochet repression after the coup lasted for a few years and would poison the Chilean political atmosphere for years to come. Pinochet had declared an amnesty in April 1978 for those who had engaged in the political crimes. However, the relatives of the *desaparecidos* continued to press for justice and the center-left governments that followed Pinochet questioned the legitimacy of the amnesty. Part of the repression in the years 1976-77 had been coordinated with other South American dictators at that time. It went under the code name of "Operation Condor." It had the objective of eliminating leftist opponents of these regimes. "Operation Condor" may have been the first example of a globalized police, or presumably "anti-terrorist," action.

I was in Rio de Janeiro on an economic mission on behalf of the OAS when the news of Allende's election was reported in 1970. That morning I had to go by taxi to a meeting when I heard the news. I have briefly mentioned this story in my previous chapters on Brazil, but here I would like to further discuss its implications for Chile. In the taxi I started a conversation with the taxi driver in my broken Portuguese and asked his reaction to Allende's election. The taxi driver was poorly dressed, and the taxi was old and in bad shape. These elements contributed to my surprise at the answer. The driver said, "Look, I own this taxi jointly with my brother-in-law. I drive it for 12 hours a day and my brother-in-law drives it for another 12 hours. We don't make much money. But the taxi is our own and the money we make is our money. I play the lottery every week. Suppose I win. Do you think that it would be fair for someone like Allende to take away my money?" Obviously Allende's leftist reputation had preceded his election. At that point I concluded that Allende would have no chance to be elected in Brazil. I also understood why in spite of its poverty, crime, and poor income distribution, Brazil never had a truly significant communist party or widespread political terrorism, as several other Latin American countries had. In the 1930s there had been some flirtation with communism that had also influenced some of the Brazilian writers, but it had not amounted to much.

The fall of Allende led to the military dictatorship of Pinochet and, for about ten years, to much economic experimentation. Chile became a laboratory for many market-oriented policies. In spite of his considerable political sins, Pinochet was apparently genuinely interested in economically modernizing the country. Many jokes circulated at the time based on what some would consider an obsession on the part of Pinochet. For this modernization, Pinochet relied on a group of mostly University of Chicago's trained economists, including some who had worked for the OAS in the early 1970s while I was working there. These included Rolf Luders and Sergio de la Quadra, among others. These economists attempted to transform the overregulated Chilean economy into an example of an ideal, market-oriented economy as promoted by the University of Chicago. After some very large, initial costs, costs that would have sent democratic policymakers packing, they achieved significant success with their reforms. Therefore, within a few years, Chile went from Allende's attempt to create a workers' paradise to Pinochet's attempt to create a capitalists' paradise!

These so-called "Chicago boys" had studied mostly with Professor Milton Friedman and Professor Arnold Harberger in Chicago. They brought a lot of imagination, energy, and theoretical knowledge, though not much real life experience, to the process of economic transformation and, as already mentioned, they made some initial costly mistakes. Eventually the changes started paying off, the economic situation settled, and Chile ended up with some of the best economic institutions of any developing country. Pinochet's support allowed the "Chicago boys" to continue with their program even though, in the short run, as in the early 1980s, it created enormous economic difficulties that would have forced more democratic regimes to change course. In time Chile, became almost a developed country with a per capita income now around US$13,000.

Over the years, in many ways, Chile became a pilot project for the rest of the developing world and even for developed countries. Other countries started noticing and copying some of its institutions. By 2006 Chile ended up with the lowest index of corruption in Latin America and, perhaps as important, with a population with a high index of economic literacy. This facilitated for the government the introduction or the continuation of good policies. The Chilean Corruption Perception Index, compiled on behalf of Transparency International, an institution in Berlin, was 7.3—just above that of the United States, and just below that of Ireland and Belgium. The index goes from 0 to 10, 10 being the best, for a country without corruption. The index for Chile was the best among Latin American countries and among developing countries. Hopefully, it will continue to retain this privileged position in future years, although in 2007 and later there has again been some concern about corruption. The Chilean experience supports the conclusion that structural and institutional reforms are not likely to generate immediate returns. Before the reforms can change the behavior of the economic agents that operate in a country and generate positive results, these agents must become convinced that the policies will not be reversed, as they often are and must not be distorted in their applications. As some economists, including Avinah Dixit of Princeton, have put it, there is often some value in waiting especially when wrong decisions cannot be reversed without major costs. But, once the reform process is complete, a country can derive substantial benefits over the long run from good reforms.

Chile's economic success, with Pinochet at the head, reinforced a school of thought that promoted enlightened dictatorship for good economic development. Proponents of this school often point to countries such as Chile under Pinochet, Korea under General Park, China, and Singapore as examples of countries that grew fast and, to some extent, were able to change their institutions under undemocratic leadership. However, the leadership must remain in place for a long time and must have clear ideas and a genuine interest in modernizing the country in order to have this kind of impact. Unfortunately, most dictators do not have clear ideas or a genuine interest in modernizing their countries. Thus their citizens lose their political freedom without any real economic gains. In conclusion, in spite of his considerable and serious political crimes, Pinochet has been credited by some for having allowed first rate economic institutions to emerge in Chile.

An interesting question is what would have happened to Chile if Allende had remained in power and had continued with his leftist experiment. Would Chile have become like Cuba or like Sweden? For sure it would be different from what it is today. We will never be able to answer that question. However, one conclusion is certain; many of the *desaparecidos* would still be around today and some aborted children would be part of today's world.

During my frequent trips to Russia and Eastern Europe after the break-up of the Soviet Union, I often heard comments that these countries should adopt "Pinochet methods" to promote fast growth. I could never understand precisely what this meant. Was it a call for the rejection of democracy? We know that many dictatorships or authoritarian governments have had disastrous results for their countries' economies. In conclusion, while Pinochet became a Devil to many, he became almost a hero to some. This supported the philosophy that I heard in Bali, and that prevails among some religions of India, that no one, not even a God, is completely evil or completely good. In fact in some religions the Devil is a God that has become bad.

Pinochet's political successors, with mild left-of-center orientations, made no attempt to substantively change the basic institutions and the economic policies created or implemented during the Pinochet's regime. The political environment changed far more than the economic environment. The acrimonious discussions of economic policies, and the sudden shifts in policies common in many countries, were largely absent in Chile in the past two decades. Over that period the country had the fastest rate of growth and the best economic performance in Latin America. It thus became truly a pilot project for many other countries, generating positive externalities in terms of good policies imitated by other countries. It also produced some effective advocates for those policies.

Some of the important changes made in Chile during the Pinochet era included the following:

(a) the privatization of the pension system, which became a model for many other countries, both developing and advanced;

(b) the privatization of most public enterprises, except those producing copper which remained in government's hands and generated a lot of revenue during the recent commodity boom;

(c) the widespread use of competent and objective cost-benefit analysis for project evaluation which made public investment more productive; the liberalization of the electricity sector that allowed a restructuring of the industry by unbundling the generation, transmission, and distribution of electricity;

(d) the widespread use of vouchers in the school system that allowed many children to go to private schools of their choice;

(e) a stabilization fund for revenue from copper exports in order to avoid cyclical shifts in public revenue and public spending. That fund has allowed Chile to have an effective built-in stabilization policy;

(f) an independent central bank;

(g) a largely independent and depoliticized tax administration and a good and stable tax system;

(h) a transparent regulatory system that has allowed the recourse to public-private partnerships for major investments in infrastructures, including the first-rate, multi-billion, transportation network built around Santiago;

(i) social expenditure targeted toward poorer social groups; and

(j) the objective application of generally transparent rules.

Chile was also one of the first developing countries to open the economy to foreign competition, to lower its tariffs, and to use a single, low and falling import duty for all imports.

The depoliticized tax administration of Chile contrasts significantly with the highly politicized tax administrations of most other Latin American countries. In these countries it is normal for high level political individuals to instruct, or to push, the tax administrators to be lenient or strict vis-à-vis particular taxpayers who are either friends or political opponents. Many Latin American countries seem to follow a famous Italian maxim: you interpret the law for your friends and apply it strictly for others.

An area where economic policy has failed so far in terms of its results, if not in terms of its effort, is income distribution. In Chile the income distribution has remained uneven, with a very high Gini coefficient. This income distribution was described as "a disgrace" by Nicolas Eyzaguirre, the Finance Minister in 2005 and a former Chilean representative at the IMF. Eyzaguirre is now back at the IMF as the director of the Western Hemisphere Department that follows the economic developments of the Americas. In spite of its efforts, Chile has not succeeded in improving significantly its income distribution, even though in absolute terms the real income of the poor has risen as a consequence of the sustained growth rate of the country. This uneven income distribution is common in Latin America, and Chile has been praised for at least trying hard to reduce income inequality. The government has not ignored the problem, but it has found that it is a difficult one to solve. Many fear that a frontal attack on the income or wealth distribution, for example with sharply progressive income or property taxes or with forced land redistribution, might have a significantly negative impact on incentives and reduce the growth rate. This is a trade-off feared by economists and often ignored or misunderstood by leftist politicians. Some years ago I had written a paper for a conference in Brazil in which I argued that there are social norms, habits, and traditions in many countries that tend to perpetuate the existing income distribution and that reduce the impact of policies that are not the radical policies that may accompany true revolutions. Chile seems to validate the conclusions of that paper.

In the past two decades, Chilean economists have been actively advising the governments of "transition economies" and of other countries how to move toward a market economy. These economists have been especially active in assisting with pension reforms which in many countries have followed what has come to be called the Chilean model. This model gives a high role to government-mandated *private* pensions, and the 2008-2009 financial crisis will surely test these policies. It remains to be seen whether they will survive. In advocating Chilean policies, these economic advisers have raised Chile's status above what one would expect from a country of its size and with its population. In 2008, a Chilean economist even became the chief economist at the OECD in Paris. These policies have been consistently pro-market. However, in the most recent years, and even before the 2008-2009 crisis, the Chilean pension model came under some criticism because of its high administrative costs and the fact that it did not cover people who did not have regular jobs. In 2005, a more socially conscious administration came into power with the intention to bring more changes than previous administrations had brought. One of its intentions was to give minimum pensions to everyone. It will be interesting to see what impact the change of administration will have on the country's long run economic policies. The current (2009) impression is that the previously unanimous support for the policies may be tested more than in past years. For example, there have been stronger pressures to dip further into the surpluses accumulated by the copper fund to support economic activities with Keynesian counter-cyclical policies. However, so far the relaxation of past policies is still limited and Chile continues to have the reputation of having the best economic policies and institutions in Latin America.

My first visit to Chile took place in 1987, when Pinochet was still in power. I visited Chile, on the way to Argentina, at the invitation of Eduardo Aninat, who later was to become Chile's Minister of Finance and, later still, a Deputy Managing Director of the IMF. At the time of my visit he was a private economic consultant. He had invited me to give a seminar on the foreign debt problem of Latin America in Santiago. After the Mexican financial crisis of 1982, when Mexico was no longer able to service its large and growing foreign debt, foreign debt became Latin America's main economic problem. Much of the 1980s, a period that came to be called the "lost decade" for Latin American countries, was focused on how to meet the foreign debt's obligations of most Latin American countries. Some Latin American countries, including Argentina, suffered real, deep, economic depressions in this period. Chile, like other Latin American countries, had a huge foreign debt problem. What came to be called the original sin of these countries, prevented them from borrowing domestically in their own currencies. For the seminar, I had expected to talk to a small informal group and was much surprised when I arrived in Santiago to find out that it had been organized at the Hilton Hotel and hundreds of people had been invited. I did my best to make my lecture interesting and argued that weak public finances had been at the origin of much of Latin America's debt problems of. Cheap foreign loans in the second half of the 1970s had often been used to increase unproductive public spending and to make bad public investments, which had not generated the hoped-for higher growth rates. The loans were generally short term and in dollar.

When the US Federal Reserve increased sharply the interest rate in the early 1980s, to fight inflation in the USA, many Latin American countries, (starting with Mexico), got caught by the increase. They could not roll over the maturing debts at the previous low rates. In some way, what happened to them, was similar to what happened to those who had bought houses in the USA in recent years at very low, initial, "teaser" rates. In 1982, in Latin America, the ratio of public investment to GDP had been particularly high, but a lot of that investment was bad investment. In my talk, I stressed that complying with foreign debt obligations would require major fiscal efforts.

The next day, Eduardo Aninat, whom I had met at Harvard and with whom I had kept contact while he was teaching at Boston University and I was working at the IMF, invited me to his farm outside of Santiago. I came to appreciate the value of Chilean agricultural land, blessed by Mediterranean weather and by seasons that are the reverse of those in the United States. I understood why Chile's national anthem contains the words: "Pure Chile is your blue-hued sky….Your fields embroidered with flowers are a joyous likeness to Eden." Chile has a North-South Pacific coastline that is more than six thousand miles long. This gives it a lot of climatic diversity. Combined with its seasonal aspect, it allows Chile to sell its beautiful fruit crops to American and increasingly European consumers during the winter months in the Northern Hemisphere. It is great to be able to eat cherries at Christmas in the cold winter. Thus, in a way, Chile gets a rent out of being in the southern hemisphere, a rent that has grown with the globalization of the world. In recent years it has started to share this rent with other countries, such as Australia, South Africa, and Argentina, countries that have similar geographic situations but not necessarily the same Mediterranean weather.

After my visit to Chile, I left for Argentina stopping in Mendoza on the way to Cordoba. I was going to Cordoba to speak at the Jornadas de Finanzas Publicas, an important academic event organized by Professor Ernesto Rezk of the University of Cordoba in Argentina. The flight over the Andes was truly spectacular because of the many tall ice-covered mountains and the blue and cloudless sky. Flying over the

Andes, I was reminded of the plane that had crashed in the mountains a few years earlier and that had not been found for several weeks. The survivors kept themselves alive by eating the dead body of a passenger's mother who, if I remember well, was a medical doctor. Thus, in a way the mother had given him life twice. Two books described the ordeal, *Miracle in the Andes* and *Alive*, the latter of which was made into a film.

In Mendoza, the passengers had to deplane for immigration controls. Here it turned out that I did not have a visa for entering Argentina on my UN passport. I had not thought that it was necessary because it was not needed for Chile. The frontier personnel did not want me to get back on the plane for Cordoba and wanted to send me back to Chile on the next available plane. I kept insisting that I must continue on the flight because that afternoon I was to be the main speaker at the meeting in Cordoba. I tried to convince them to check with the organizers of the Cordoba meeting or with the staff at the Central Bank or the Ministry of Economy of Argentina, who would know me. During this heated discussion that lasted for some time, the plane was kept waiting with the passengers on board and the engines running. Finally they decided to let me board the plane on condition that in Cordoba I immediately acquired a visa. When I boarded the plane, I was met by the applause of the passengers who were glad that the plane could leave. Undoubtedly I had cost them a lot of time, not to mention costing the airline a lot of money because of the extra fuel used. I was embarrassed by the experience.

I returned to Chile in January 1996 to speak at the annual conference on fiscal policy organized by the Economic Commission for Latin America and the Caribbean (ECLAC). I took my son, Alex, with me and made plans to visit the extreme south of Chile for a few days before the Conference. We left Washington with two feet of snow on the ground and arrived to Santiago in the middle of the summer. These extreme contrasts in temperature always create problems on what to wear for a trip. There was not a cloud in the sky when we reached Santiago, and the temperature was a balmy 85 degrees Fahrenheit. Professor Eric Haindl, a good friend and Professor of Economics at the Gabriela Mistral University, met us at the airport. He had been a consultant for the Fiscal Affairs Department of the IMF and had been on some technical assistance missions with me. As was the case with many Chilean economists, his Ph.D. is from the University of Chicago. The Gabriela Mistral University is a private university literally "owned" by a rather formidable lady, Alicia Romo. She had been in charge of dismantling the price controls, set in place by the Allende governments, during Pinochet's military government. I was told that she had performed that job with a vengeance. She was the rector of the University.

After checking in at the Sheraton and resting for a while, Eric picked us up and took us to a luncheon at the university given in my honor by Rector Romo. About ten professors including a professor visiting from MIT, attended the luncheon. Rector Romo was obviously the authority at the university; she owned about eighty percent of all its assets. She was a firm believer in the virtue of the private sector. I was told that she had even refused public scholarship money to which the university was entitled. She did not want to be contaminated by the public sector's direct or even indirect influences. She believed that accepting any public money implied losing some freedom. The luncheon was lively and pleasant. It was obvious that Rector Romo and the professors were very proud of their university and of its status as a fully private institution.

The phenomenon of private universities is a relatively new and interesting one in Latin America. Over recent decades, the combination of leftist ideology and populism had lowered the standards of public universities, some of which had even had a prestigious historical background such as the University of San Marcos in Lima (Peru), one of the oldest university in the Americas. The market value of a public university education had significantly been reduced, caused by the obsession with accepting anyone who applied and with letting almost anyone who had the stamina to follow the courses and take the exams graduate. Some terrorist groups had infiltrated the public universities and had found them a fertile recruiting ground. As a consequence, in countries like Argentina, Chile, Mexico, and Peru, private universities were created to generate graduates that were more attractive to employers. Some of these private universities were expensive and prestigious. Others were less so. Still, many of them were thriving institutions especially in fields such as economics, business administration, accounting and other similar fields in which the operating costs are lower. Expensive and politically neutral faculties, such as medicine and engineering, were left to the public universities. Thus there was some element of skimming on the part of the private universities. This trend toward the privatization of higher learning institutions is likely to continue.

In the afternoon Haindl took us for a tour of Santiago. There are no major historical tourist attractions in Santiago because frequent earthquakes have destroyed some of the historical buildings. In any case, Chile and Santiago had never been as historically central as Peru, Cuzco and Lima. Other Latin American cities tend to be more interesting for a tourist. In the early afternoon we went to Haindl's house, where we had been invited for dinner. The house was outside the city and, to my surprise, it was just spectacular. Built on a site with a truly remarkable view of the mountains, it had been designed by Haindl's sister-in-law, who was an architect and a builder. The garden climbed to the top of a small mountain so that he could claim that he owned part of a mountain. We enjoyed meeting his wife and daughter, both named Ana Luisa, and enjoyed touring the interior of the house and the various rooms each with a beautiful view of the mountains. Even the bathrooms had such a view. The house was built in the shape of a pentagon so that each part would have a different perspective and a different view of the mountains. My friends are also collectors, so the interior of their house was also full of unusual objects collected from various places.

We sat on the veranda and had *pisco sour* and hors d'oeuvres of sea urchins, that delicacy much appreciated by Italians and Japanese but unavailable in the United States. I could not help but feel sorry for the Americans who do not eat sea urchins but, instead, sell them to the Japanese. What a loss! Mrs. Haindl had prepared a very good dinner all based on sea food, some of which was cooked, and some raw. We had a delicious serving of some kind of shellfish, which we ate raw. My son Alex, who normally does not like seafood, finished all that was served to him and enjoyed it a lot.

This visit took place at a time when the Italian movie *Il Postino* was a big success in Italy. The film dealt with the exile of Pablo Neruda, the famous Chilean poet who won the Nobel Prize in literature and who some consider the greatest poet of the twentieth century. Neruda's poems of the sea are particularly beautiful. Some have been set to music by an American composer who dedicated them to his wife, who is a famous mezzo-soprano. I had expected that the movie would have also been popular in Chile but was surprised to find out that it was not. Perhaps the influence of Pinochet was still strong at that time. Neruda had been exiled for his leftist views. I recently bought a beautiful book, *America, My Brother, My Blood*, which combines some of the poems by Pablo Neruda with the paintings of Oswaldo Guayasamin.

CHAPTER 10

CHILE: A VISIT TO PATAGONIA

The morning after this splendid seafood dinner, my son and I went to the airport to catch our plane to Punta Arena, the southernmost city of the American continent. The flight, on a Lan Chile jet, lasted a bit more than three hours, headed directly south. The plane was full and the service very good. Lan Chile, a private enterprise, was trying to establish a reputation for service and safety that would make it possible to survive without subsidies in a very competitive industry. From the plane we could admire spectacular views of lakes, mountains, deserts, glaciers, and especially volcanoes. Chile has six hundred volcanoes, sixty of which are still active. We learned that the mountain range of the Andes grows a centimeter per year thanks to these volcanoes. The weather was beautiful all the way and similar to the kind of weather one gets over the Mediterranean Sea in the summer. Looking outside of the window of the plane, I could understand why, in the sixteenth century, Pedro de Valdivia had invited his Spanish countrymen to settle in Chile "because there is no better place in the world to live." Pedro de Valdivia is considered the conqueror of Chile. He and his small band of Spanish conquerors established the city of Santiago in 1541. However, the conquerors had a difficult time controlling the territory because of the continuing hostility of the indigenous people, the Mapuche. The Mapuche offered stiff resistance to the conquerors, and it was not until 1883 that the new occupants of Chile definitively defeated them.

We arrived in Punta Arena on time and were met by our guide, Ricardo. We transferred our suitcases into Ricardo's car and began the trip to our hotel. Apparently the Incas named this land Chile, even though there are various theories about its origin. For the Incas it meant the end of the land or, the end of the world, or "the deepest point of the Earth." Thus, while China's original name means the center of the world, Chile's means the end of it. It surely must have seemed to be the end of the world to those who crossed into the American continent from Asia. I could not believe that one could fly straight south, in a jet, for more than three hours from Santiago without leaving the continent. I had always considered Santiago, with Buenos Aires and Montevideo, as the southernmost American cities. But then I reminded myself that Chile has a coast line of more than 6000 miles, twice the width of the United States. When you get to Punta Arena, it indeed feels like this is where the world ends. The only place you can fly south from there is Antarctica. In the summer, there are flights from Punta Arena to a Chilean base in Antarctica and more and more tourists have been going there. While waiting for our suitcases, it did occur to me that I might like to fly to Antarctica. This thought must have come from the Marco Polo hidden inside of me. I communicated this thought to Alex, and he simply shook his head and thought I was crazy.

Punta Arena is right on the Magellan Strait in the appropriately named Magellan Province. The Magellan Strait had a period of some economic importance before the Panama Canal was built. It is a very windy and cold place and not easy to navigate because of frequent storms. Magellan had a terrible time making his way from the Atlantic to the Pacific. One can again turn to Lawrence Bergreen's *Over the Edge of the World* for more information on this. Before the Panama Canal opened in 1914, the Magellan Strait was the only way to get from the Atlantic to the Pacific Ocean by sea, making it a crucial thoroughfare. Now only an occasional supertanker uses it. Punta Arena has major unemployment and provides little hope for its young people. At least at the time of our visit this part of Chile was not benefiting from the growth of the Chilean economy. The government had provided tax incentives to the area, but geography surely seems to work against this region. It is just too far from anywhere.

On the way to the hotel we stopped at a little café where the tourist attraction, however few tourists there were, was a captive condor. The condor is an enormous bird with a wingspan of six feet or more. It is also a scavenger. I took a few pictures of the poor fellow, who was captured before he could fly and thus never learned to fly. Further along our route, we saw many burned trees and were told that many years earlier, in the 1920s, the price of wool was very high and farmers had tried to clear the land to raise more sheep. Raising sheep is the only productive use for this land because it is not arable due to high winds, low temperatures for much of the year, and low fertility. When the price of wool fell during the Great Depression, these marginal lands were abandoned. These large areas marked by burned trees make a striking site.

On our journey, we stopped at Puerto Natales, the second largest city in the region, with a population of about 22,000. It is largely a tourist town where visitors can take a boat ride to the glaciers. Puerto Natales looks a bit like a Swiss town with chalets. It is in a province called La Última Esperanza, or the Last Hope. The name must be indicative of something, but I am not sure what. We had a hot chocolate in the lobby of a hotel, filled up with gas, and moved on. The road was not particularly spectacular until we got closer to the Parque Nacional Torres del Paine. As we entered the park, we had our first encounter with Patagonian foxes. Four or five foxes were playing not far from us, and they did not seem too impressed by our presence. I took several pictures of them. We also saw large groups of *guanacos*, a wild variety of llama and an extremely graceful animal. They generally move in large groups and run away when one tries to approach them.

The road got progressively more interesting, and we finally arrived at Lake Pehoé. Our hotel, the Hosteria Pehoé is on a small island right in the middle of the lake. A narrow, long, wooden foot bridge connects it with the mainland. It would be a great understatement to say that the landscape is spectacular. Just imagine a lake of the bluest water coming directly from huge glaciers located in the surrounding mountains. The Massiccio del Paine, the Cuernos del Paine, and the Torres del Paine are among the most beautiful mountains that one can imagine. They look like French *baguettes* rising straight up out of the ground. From the hotel dining room, one can see Lake Pehoé and its backdrop of massive mountains, which are very difficult to climb given that at some points they are practically vertical and they are buffeted by high winds. Many climbers have lost their lives trying to climb them. Where the mountains are not vertical, they are covered with massive glaciers which from time to time break and come crushing down with the sound of thunder. The mountains resemble those that one sees in Guilin in China and in Chinese traditional paintings.

The Hosteria had only eighteen rooms, going for about US$100 per night. The rooms were very small and Spartan but the location of the hotel compensated for it. The staff was friendly and the food was fine. The car had to park on the other side of the bridge so that the suitcases had to be hand carried over the long bridge. Within the Torres del Paine National Park there are a few other hotels, all of which are small and well situated. Some of the others were more expensive than the Hosteria Pehoé. At least one hotel, the Hotel Explora, was very expensive.

The next day we started with a nice breakfast at the Hosteria. Then, led by Ricardo, we climbed a small mountain not far from the hotel. We climbed about 1500 feet to a vista point overlooking four lakes: the Grey, the Pehoé, the Sarmiento, and the Nordenskjold. There was not a cloud in the sky, and the temperature was about 55 degrees Fahrenheit. I found the climb a bit hard for my age, and when we got to the top my heart was beating in a way it was not used to. I perspired as I rarely do in spite of the cool temperature. I also suffer a bit from vertigo, but still I persevered, and the result justified the effort. The flora was also spectacular, with magnificent flowers of all kinds and many plants that I had never seen before. We sat on top—though really at the bottom— of the world for about an hour contemplating the scenery. Neither I nor my son wanted to talk. We did not want to be distracted from this incredible place and time. I remembered a quote by the Italian writer Cesare Pavese that one does not remember days but moments. This was surely a moment to remember.

After we had fully absorbed the beautiful spectacle that nature had offered us, we started the descent. We got to the car and drove along the Rio Paine to the Sede Administrativa, the Administrative Office of the Park, where we saw a map of the Park and looked at some information on the local flora and fauna. We learned that the main predators in the area are pumas, foxes, and condors. We also learned that hikers frequently get lost and must be rescued by park police. As an economist, I could not fail to ask whether rescuing them was a legitimate role of the state and whether the knowledge that the police was there to rescue them made hikers more careless. It was a classic example of what economists call a "moral hazard problem." This problem is encountered when the existence of a system of protection including an insurance makes an individual less careful.

Our next destination was the Lago Grey, from which one can see the immense Glacier Grey. However, there was a problem. A few weeks earlier, the wooden bridge over the Grey River that we needed to cross had burned down. The Grey River was not very wide, perhaps ninety feet wide, but the water moved at the speed of a torrent. We left the car near the river and crossed the very fast river in a boat that used the power of the current and a steel rope strung across the river to move the boat to the other side. The current pushed the boat with great force but the steel rope held the boat and allowed it to move slowly to the other side. One just hoped that the rope would not break. The crossing was very rapid and the cost $2.50 per person. The owner of the boat was obviously making a small fortune as a result of the fire, which made me suspicious that the fire may not have been an accident. As an economist, I could see a strong incentive to set the fire. Besides, how does a bridge catch fire? Another beneficiary was the owner of a bus that just happened to be on the right side of the river when the fire occurred. Both of these beneficiaries had acquired monopoly powers after the fire and they were using it to the maximum to make a fast buck. We paid the bus to take us the 11 miles to the Hosteria Lago Grey, a small, nice, modern hotel with a beautiful view of the lake and the glacier.

At the Hosteria, we had a nice lunch of Peruvian eggs, salmon, and watermelon and then walked to the Lake. We had to walk about half an hour to get to the shore, and then almost another mile on a gravelly road to get to the water. In the summer, the lake shrinks, exposing an enormous beach. By now it had become very windy with some gusts easily exceeding fifty miles per hour. The beach was full of pieces of old wood that had been worn down into unusual shapes by the glacier and the river. Perhaps stimulated by the unusual environment, in my imagination I could see faces and animals in the pieces of wood and I took many pictures of them. It was as if, in a form of animism, many creatures had found their places in the objects around us. There was a spooky feeling about this place. I kept trying to bring this to my son's attention. Alex, who is not the poetic type, or is perhaps just less imaginative, gave me looks of commiseration which meant, my father is going bananas!

We followed a path that led to a kind of promontory overlooking the lake. Immediately after that promontory the lake becomes the Grey River, which moves at great speed. We had to climb up a very narrow goat's path with the strong wind blowing, and I was afraid that the wind would blow me into the frigid lake. The lake was full of large pieces of ice that had detached from the huge, nearby glacier. The ice was the most incredible blue and formed all kinds of beautiful sculptures. It truly was nature's art at its best and posed a strong challenge to man-made art. Normally a boat would take visitors near the glacier, but on that day the wind was too strong and the boat rides had been cancelled. Still, the whole trip was tremendously worthwhile though tiring. We had to wait some time at the Hosteria Lago Grey for the bus that would take us back to our car at the river's crossing. I took advantage of this time to take more photos. The long trip back to the hotel was pleasant and uneventful.

The next day, we left the hotel at 9:30. Our destination was Salto Grande, or The Big Jump, one of three falls we visited. At the Salto Grande, the Lake Nordenskjold spills into the Lake Pehoé which eventually becomes the Paine River. It is interesting here to see the birth of lakes and rivers. The Salto Grande is a large and powerful fall in a narrow canyon. The water moves at an incredible speed, and the sight is stunning. From the Salto Grande we walked for more than an hour to an observation point on Lake Nordenskjold. From there we were facing the Glacier Frances of the Mountain Paine Grande and the Cuervos del Paine. We were close enough to see the cracks in the ice and to hear the rumble of occasional avalanches. We could also admire the various creeks or falls that feed the lake. This was puma territory and, although I had been assured that they do not attack people, I must confess that I had some apprehension. I knew that in other parts of the world including California they occasionally do attack people, and the thought of being eaten alive was not a pleasant one. We did not see any pumas but we saw some of their footprints. The guide told us that they sleep during this time of the day.

From the Salto Grande we drove to the Refugio Laguna Amarga, where we had a quick lunch with sandwiches that had been packed at the hotel for the trip. I discovered that the Rio Paine actually starts at Lake Paine, then it becomes Lake Nordenskjold which falls at Salto Grande into Lake Pehoé to become Rio Paine. After the lunch we proceeded toward the Cascada Paine, or the Paine Falls. On the drive, we could see the opposite sides of the mountains from the ones we had seen from the hotel and the various mountains that form the Torres del Paine. These are mountains that look like towers having almost perpendicular walls. I could not stop being amazed by the beauty of these mountains. Again they reminded me of the mountains in Guilin in China, although the Chilean mountains are taller.

Along the way we saw a large group of *guanacos* grazing near a small lake. They always showed curiosity combined with apprehension when we stopped to look at them. While we were admiring these graceful animals, some movement overhead attracted my attention and that of a few other visitors. We looked up and saw about twenty condors flying over our heads in fluid, graceful movements. As they are scavengers, they must have sensed that perhaps one of the *guanacos* was in trouble and they were looking forward to a feast. I took some pictures of these magnificent birds in flight and followed them to a rendezvous point at the top of a hill. This must have been a good observatory for them.

We continued on to Cascada Paine that turned out to be a spectacular view. The speed of the river was tremendous, and the water divided around a huge and very attractive rock. At the back the view of the mountains was magnificent, and the sight of the fall was also lovely with lots of wildflowers growing among burned tree trunks. Signs of forest fires could be seen everywhere with burned trees almost constantly in sight. Apparently fires are often started by campers when they burn wood for cooking or when they throw lighted cigarette butts into the dry wood. We were told that now guards are more attentive to fires and there were many signs warning visitors to be more careful. We completed the day by going to the Salto Chico near the Explora Hotel. It was a nice sight but not as spectacular as the others we had seen.

During our four days in the Parque Nacional, the weather was generally good, although it changed frequently. The sky was variable but always beautiful. The sun was very strong but so was the wind, and when a cloud covered the sun, one felt immediately cold. The clouds were different in shape and color from those we see in the North. At one point I recall seeing several concentric saucers one on top of the other. If I believed in UFOs, I would have sworn that they were flying saucers, but they were clouds. The flora was always extraordinary with many bushes and flowers that we had not seen before. The color of the water in the lakes and in the river was of the most profound green or blue that one can imagine. This pristine land felt different in some fundamental way from other places. I had the same feeling when I had visited the Argentine side of Patagonia.

On our last day we got up early to leave for Punta Arenas, where we would get our flight back to Santiago. It would take five to six hours to get to Punta Arenas. The entrance to the Parque, and the exit from it, opens at 8:30 so that we were at the gate right on time to go out. Once again we enjoyed the fantastic scenery. For a short while before leaving the hotel, there was no wind and Lake Pehoé became a perfect mirror for the surrounding mountains. It was almost a kind of beautiful, impressionistic painting. Of course, I took several photos. Once again we saw many of the local animals, such as *guanacos*, foxes, wild rabbits, and large mountain birds that looked like ostriches.

For a good part of the two-lane road to the airport, only the right lane was paved while the left lane was covered with gravel and small stones. The result was that every vehicle, regardless of which direction it was going, stayed in the right lane. Those who should have been on the left side of the road, those moving toward us, waited until the last minute to move to their unpaved side. This would happen while both vehicles were moving toward each other at seventy or eighty miles an hour! If the vehicles coming from the opposite direction were large, such as buses or trucks, they would delay the move so that a game of chicken was played: they tried to force the smaller ones, which were on their rightful side of the road, to squeeze as far as they could to the right. On the road to the airport, I was impressed by the number of small altars on the side of the road dedicated to people who had died in traffic accidents. I was also impressed by the dangers that an almost empty road can present to drivers when they drive carelessly at very high speeds.

One particularly noteworthy altar was decorated with literally hundreds of empty, multicolored bottles and plastic containers. In an area where there are few real flowers for most of the year, this rainbow of colors provided a substitute to keep the dead in good spirits. The plastic containers and bottles, some of which might have been colored on purpose, were strung together with rope, so as to stay in place and not be scattered by the high winds. This particular accident victim must have been important or much loved, judging from the richness of the altar.

We were forced to stop twice due to animal crossings. The first of these crossings consisted of a large number of cows guided by sheep dogs and by a *gaucho*, or cowboy, on horseback. The dogs were very busy in forcing a few stray cows to fall into place. The second crossing was far more colorful—or actually colorless because of the limited color range. It involved literally thousands of sheep crossing the road. Once again much of the work was being done by the sheepdogs while the gaucho on horseback mostly watched. I had never seen so many sheep and been so close to them. They kept coming toward our car in close formation. They were so crowded together that they all touched one another leaving no space between them. It was really gorgeous to see this multitude of creatures advance for several minutes while feeling completely safe. I wondered what they would do if, instead of being in a car, we were standing outside. Would they go around us or knock us down and step over us? I would not like to find out. Unfortunately, my son had packed his camcorder in the trunk so that he could not film this rather remarkable scene. I had time to take several shots, although my camera at the time was refusing to function properly because of the lack of color contrast. One of the photos that I took of the sheep won an honorable mention at the annual photographic exhibition of the World Bank and the IMF.

At the airport we found out that our flight was going to be at least one hour late. While we were having something to eat at the airport restaurant, a voice came on the loudspeaker and asked me to contact Lan Chile. When I lifted the phone, there was the woman on the line from the Hosteria on the lake where we had stayed. She had apparently given me both receipts of the payment I had made to settle my hotel bill. Very graciously she asked if I could leave the pink copy with Lan Chile so that they could send someone to pick it up. She explained that they needed the tax receipt to settle their value added tax obligations.

This call was the best sign for me that the tax system works in Chile. I was reminded then of a story I had heard about the head of the tax administration's visit to Pinochet when Pinochet was the head of the Chilean government. I could not verify if it was a true story or a piece of political propaganda distributed by the Pinochet regime. Pinochet was told by the head of the tax administration that his brother, a shop owner, had been caught cheating on his taxes and was asked what the tax administration should do. Pinochet asked two questions:

First, are you sure?

Answer: yes, no question! We have proofs.

Second, what is the normal punishment for this type of tax evasion?

Answer: a fine and the closing of the shop for a given period of time.

Pinochet: then go and apply the full sanction as you would for any taxpayer.

Too bad that the value of this story was spoiled later by the news that Pinochet had had a secret bank account with the Riggs Bank in Washington. This news was a great delusion for his followers, who had thought of him as authoritarian but personally honest.

Returning to Santiago after my trip to the South, I participated in the "Annual Conference on Fiscal Policy" organized by the United Nation's Economic Commission for Latin America and the Caribbean (ECLAC) or CEPAL in Spanish. Juan Carlos Lerda, an Argentine economist working with ECLAC at that time, had initiated these annual conferences, and they were becoming more important every year. I attended a few of them, before leaving the IMF at the end of 2000. They were attracting participants from many Latin American countries, including high level government officials. That year the conference was on "quasi-fiscal activities" (QFA) and on regulations. QFAs are actions that have effects similar to those of government spending and taxes but that are often carried out by institutions other than the government proper. Often they are carried out through regulations. For example, public enterprises might be required to provide services to particular customers even when the enterprises would suffer losses. Or central banks might be required to provide cheap credit to some sectors of the economy, such as agriculture. My lecture, given in Spanish, was well received, and I was proud of my Spanish in spite of its high content of Italian. The second day of the conference I gave a brief talk on globalization and taxes, a subject in which I had recently written a book for Brookings, a Washington Think Tank, and several articles.

The CEPAL headquarters is very nice and the conference was attended by high level officials from most Latin American countries. It took place in a conference room named after Raul Prebisch, who had been the director general of the ECLAC for many years. Prebisch had been a very influential Argentine economist who in the 1950s had convinced the policymakers of several Latin American countries to pursue policies that would restrict imports through high tariffs or through prohibitions of imports. He believed that this would stimulate the domestic production of those goods and promote Latin America's industrialization and development. He also believed this would reduce the Latin American countries' dependency on commodity exports. At the time a prevalent concern was that the prices of commodities were subjected to a declining historical trend. At the meeting I discussed the likelihood of Cuba rejoining the IMF with Cuba's Deputy Minister of Finance and listened to the changes that were taking place in Nicaragua after its Sandinista period. Interestingly Ortega, the head of the Sandinistas, would democratically return to power in 2006 after winning the election.

I visited Eduardo Aninat, who had become Chile's Minister of Finance. He was remarkably relaxed for a minister of finance, perhaps because he was on his way to the annual World Development Forum in Davos, Switzerland, and then to a vacation. He might also have been relaxed because Chile had become an easy country to manage for a finance minister. We discussed the importance of social policy in developing countries and the difficulty of making that policy successfully improve the distribution of income. This was a topic that would worry both of us for years to come. I had organized two conferences at the IMF on this topic, which had been attended by prominent economists including Nobel Prize winners and had resulted in two good books. Aninat pointed to the importance of reducing public debt in order to allocate the resources saved on servicing the debt to social programs.

When I came out of Aninat's office, I was surrounded by a group of reporters who took pictures of me and asked a few questions. I gave diplomatic and bland answers for a couple of minutes, but they still managed to write long articles in the following day's newspapers. In these interviews I was often embarrassed by my answers, which were fairly banal because I was concerned that I would say something I might regret or that would embarrass the IMF. Still, the reporters at times managed to report them as if I had said something truly novel or radical.

In 2005, Chile elected the first woman to become president of a Latin American country on her own right and not through succession, Michelle Bachelet. She is a physician and the daughter of a general who had opposed Pinochet and had been tortured by the regime. She herself had spent some years in exile. She brought a first-rate economist, who had been a professor at the Harvard Kennedy School, as Minister of Finance. Andres Velasco would be a guarantee that the good economic policies followed by Chile in recent years would continue and, where necessary, be adjusted. The very high price for copper in recent years gave Chile a huge revenue windfall and raised pressures on the government to spend the extra revenue immediately rather than to save it for rainy days when the price of copper might come down as it did in 2009. These windfalls, associated with commodity booms, have often led Latin American countries to large increases in public spending which could not be easily reversed when the export prices fell. Thus, these changes in prices, created major economic problems for some of these countries. This behavior made fiscal policy pro-cyclical rather than counter-cyclical, as it should be.

In October 2006, I went back to Santiago for a conference at the headquarters of the Economic Commission for Latin America and the Caribbean (ECLAC or CEPAL). The conference was part of a program,

Redima, or Red de Investigacion Macroeconomica, financed by the European Union. I had been asked to write a paper on macroeconomic development in Latin America. My wife, Maria, accompanied me. I presented the paper to participants from ministries of finance and central banks of Latin American countries. My paper argued against the accumulation of public debt even to finance the building of infrastructure. This position went against that being promoted by some economists, policymakers, and even some international organizations. They were arguing that Latin America had developed a major "infrastructure gap" and that this gap was a major cause of the continent's slow rate of growth. They argued that fiscal concerns, such as high fiscal deficits and public debts, should not be reasons for not borrowing for public investments. Presumably the public investments would make the countries grow faster and thus automatically and painlessly solve the fiscal problems created by borrowing. In my paper I argued that these very policies had led to the fiscal and debt crises of the 1980s, the "lost decade" for Latin America. Public investment in Latin America had reached the record level of 7.5 percent of GDP in 1982, the year when the decade's debt crisis started. Public investment had been financed by foreign loans at that time.

After the conference, I visited Vittorio Corbo, then the President of the Central Bank whom I had known for many years when he was at the World Bank and I was at the IMF. He was satisfied with the Chilean economic policy and felt that the new administration would not bring significant changes to the country's prudent macroeconomic policy. He did admit, however, that some adjustments were likely to be made to the country's social policy in order to reflect the more leftist preferences of the new president.

The next day my wife and I took an early flight with Lan Chile to fly to Calama, the town from which we would go by car to San Pedro de Atacama. San Pedro is in the middle of the Atacama desert, one of the most arid deserts in the world. There are parts of it where it has never rained and other parts where if, it rains, it is a few millimeters per year. The trip from Calama to San Pedro is a little over sixty miles of pure desert. My imagination had associated deserts with flat areas and a lot of golden sand, but this desert was far from being flat except for a salt lake and its color did not resemble that of gold. Its landscape was also extraordinarily varied. Within the Atacama desert, a large area is covered by the Salar de Atacama, or the Atacama Salt Flat, located between the Andes and the Domeyco Mountain Range. Two tiny rivers, the San Pedro and the Vilama, cross the area. They carry little water from the mountains because the water flows mostly to the East, toward the Amazon Basin. The area's ecological floor varies from 7500 feet above sea level to about 20000 feet. This variation creates sharp changes in temperature and unforgettable sights. Because of the high altitude, we were advised to take it easy the first day. Thus we planned the tours for the following days.

The Atacama Desert has been occupied by humans for about twelve thousand years, and the Tulor area within it shows signs of three thousand year old stable settlements, normally in small oases in the middle of the desert. The round mud houses of the original inhabitants are still there, some restored. It is incredible that humans could live in this area, and it is equally incredible that some plants or even some trees manage to grow. Their roots must go deep enough to find underground water. In one area we saw a forest of large trees the roots of which, we were told, went down to a depth twice the height of the trees.

The town of San Pedro de Atacama occupies an oasis in the middle of the desert. A small river flows through it. It is a little town of about five thousand inhabitants, strategically located for the many daily excursions that can be planned for the surrounding areas. It has been receiving an increasing number of tourists from Europe, South America and other areas. As the knowledge spreads of the incredible sights within a day trips from San Pedro, it becomes more and more a tourist town but, so far, it has not lost the charm of small towns. The roads are not paved and are lined by buildings made mostly of mud. There are colorful places in which one can eat relatively simple meals. It is still far enough that relatively few people visit it. The hotels have maintained a primitive look. The one where we stayed, the Hotel Tulor, was owned by an archeologist and had rooms that were essentially circular huts with straw roofs. Due to the lack of rain the straw roofs were sufficient. The huts were designed to resemble the ones that we would see at the archeological site, Tulor, which bears the same name as the hotel.

San Pedro was founded in 1540, not many years after the Spanish first arrived in Peru. The first Spaniards arrived in this area in 1536. They imposed Christianity on the indigenous people and prohibited the Atacamenos, the indigenous people, from using their native language of *cunza*. Before the Spanish arrived, the Incas had already come to this place claiming payment of taxes in the form of work. They had had some impact on the religions and on the customs of the Atacamenos. The area of San Pedro had originally been part of Bolivia, but Bolivia lost it to Chile after the Pacific War of 1879. As a result, Bolivia lost its access to the sea and this has been a continuing thorn in the relations between the two countries, also because the area is rich in copper. I asked one of the local guides if he felt Chilean or Bolivian and I got a diplomatic reply. He said that he felt both. Recently there has been a proposal by some Chilean architects to build a 90 mile long tunnel that would allow Bolivians access to the sea without technically touching Chile. I am not sure that it is a good idea.

Our hotel was conveniently located in the town so that we did not need a car to get around. We found the town very primitive and very charming at the same time. We visited a small but lovely museum named after a Belgian priest, Gustavo Le Paige, who had spent many years in this town and had collected most of the archeological items that were shown in the museum. In the little plaza where the museum is located, there is also a small and charming Catholic church. From the hotel to the little plaza we followed the main street, which had mud buildings on both sides. On the main street we had some of our meals in a restaurant called La Estaka. It was colorful with original primitive decorations on the walls. Strangely, it played mostly big band jazz. There were several similar restaurants so that one could choose. The town of San Pedro is conveniently located close to some incredibly interesting tourist attractions. There are several tourist agencies where one can make arrangements for daily excursions by small buses.

For the first day we had made arrangements to visit "Coyote Lookout" and the surrounding area. "Coyote Lookout" is an elevated area that looks down to the most desolate valley one can imagine; nothing grows in it and there are signs of salt everywhere. After spending some time looking down on the huge valley, imagining life in this place, and taking some photos, we drove to another even more desolate area appropriately called Death Valley. A short canyon takes one to another observatory that looks down on Death Valley. The observatory was characterized by very high wind. Death Valley seemed even more desolate, more arid and more salty than the valley we had seen from the Coyote Lookout. It is not likely that anything could survive in that environment.

From Death Valley we drove to a huge salt mine, where we visited large caverns and small hills made completely of salt. We also visited a wide open area where there were several natural salt "sculptures." The various shapes reminded one of people and animals. They resembled man-made monuments. Three of these "sculptures" some 10 feet tall have been named the "Tres Marias," or Three Marias, because they vaguely resemble three women. The next stop was at the Valley of the Moon, an area where nature has reproduced truly incredible sights. In this area the prevailing color is that of gold. A group of dunes resembled a large amphitheater or a small walled city. Another resembled a golden lake. The smooth sand seemed to have become liquid gold. It had been made very smooth by the wind. We climbed up a steep hill from where we observed the most spectacular sunset that we had ever seen. We were situated on a narrow platform that was the ridge of a gold colored hill. It almost resembled the Great Wall of China. In front of us, but far below, there was another very nicely shaped and very long hill. It looked like a long, triangular, elongated bridge that moved straight away from us. It was also made of golden sand, was very smooth, and the ridge at the top of it was very narrow. A few people were walking on it, getting away from us, in order to reach another hill almost a mile away from us. The narrow path looked like a long bridge over a lake made of molten gold. The daring visitors walking on it walked as if it were a normal path. As they got farther away from us they looked more and more like small ants in the great empty vastness. The clouds were magnificent and had colors and shapes that I had not seen before. The sand in front of us was so smooth that it gave the impression of being a golden lake.

The day had been truly extraordinary and almost extraterrestrial. I do not believe I have ever had such a strong impression of being on another planet. I had seen perhaps more beautiful places but never places more alien than this. The guide, Aaron, was a young American from Oklahoma. He had come to Chile to study Spanish and had fallen in love with the place. The fact that he spoke English gave him some advantage because he could guide English speaking groups.

We had made arrangements for a second full day. We left early in the morning with a small bus and a different guide and drove to a green valley that had all kinds of fruits and even a forest right in the middle of the desert. This forest was made possible by the fact that the narrow valley was far below the level of the surrounding desert area. A creek that flowed through the valley enabled this miraculous forest and orchard to exist right in the middle of the desert. This is an area that receives over three hundred days of sunshine and no rain. Combined with the underground water that formed the creek, this sunlight could generate a lot of plush vegetation. In this area, a consortium of American universities is building a powerful telescope with the help of Japanese, Canadian and Chilean money. It is a project that will cost billions of dollars and that will allow better space exploration due to the lack of clouds, humidity, and radio interference in this area.

The next stop was the Salar de Atacama. It extends about 55 miles, making it the third largest salt lake in the world, after the Salt Lake in the USA and one in Bolivia. It is surrounded by tall mountains including active volcanoes, one of which had erupted in April 2006. The lake has formed a salt crust that allows one to walk safely on it. I had never seen so much salt in my life. We walked on the surface of the lake and approached an area in the middle of it where the salt water is not covered by hard salt. In this water bright pink flamingos had made their headquarter. We were told that their pink color comes from the fact that their main food is shrimps. There were a lot of these beautiful birds and we admired them while the sun was going down. It was again an incredible sunset, but the lack of clouds made it less spectacular than the one we had seen the previous night. We took a lot of photos and were sorry when we had to start our journey back to the town. It was strange for me to think that this area, at least 10,000 feet above sea level, had at one time been covered by sea water. It made me think about global warming and its potential impact on the world.

For the third day we had signed up for another remarkable tour that I will remember well as long as I live. The bus picked us up at 4 a.m. and was full in spite of the early hour. We had been told to eat little the night before and to take winter clothes because we would go to an area some 16,000-17,000 feet above sea level where it would be very cold. The bus followed a rough mountain road and after a couple of hours reached an area called Tatio. It was very cold, well below freezing temperature. Tatio is a large area made characteristic by many geysers and pools of boiling or hot water. It reminded me of Yellowstone, and I had the impression of walking the Earth as it must have been millions of years ago. When the sun came up it gave a magnificent color to the sight. Huge mountains, some covered with snow, surrounded the area. There was an area with a large thermal pool, and several people went into it. They had to undress in sub-freezing temperature but then they enjoyed the warm bath. We did a lot of walking and took many pictures. There were many sights with unusual flowers and plants and others where the chemicals in the water coming out of the ground had formed little sculptures or even little fountains that looked like small colorful monuments. We walked for a long time exploring various areas and enjoying the sunrise and the views. It was just a fantastic area, and we were sorry when the time came to begin our return. Remarkably the very high altitude had not been a problem although we had to walk very slowly.

On the return trip, our route took us to a little village near another desert oasis. There were few people in the village. It had a very small, but very colorful church. There was a little shop where local women were frying some *frittelle*, little pieces of dough. We bought some, and found them very tasty. In front of the village there was a small creek that created a magnificent, green valley in which some graceful *llamas* and *vicuñas* were grazing. It was a perfect spot for photos. We had a fascinating trip home over mountain roads, passing areas where geological developments had created large and unusual rock formations. We got back tired but excited from what we had seen. That night we had dinner in a different restaurant of which I do not recall the name. A Bolivian band played typical Bolivian music and they convinced us to buy one of their CDs.

The last day was perhaps the least interesting although it was still worthwhile. We arranged a tour to an old fortress called Pukar Quitor. It was far, and when we arrived there we discovered that we had a lot of climbing to do, on the side of a steep hill, to reach the fortress. It was hot, and the climbing was hard. What was left of the fortress that had dominated the valley below were some walls and a lot of large stones. It was difficult to imagine how the fortress must have looked and what its function must have been. Although both the Incas and the Spanish came, it is difficult to image who would want to come this way. It was also difficult to determine where the occupants of the fortress got their water. During this tour we visited the archeological site of Tulor, the establishment that had existed three thousand years ago. The people there had lived in little circular mud huts sharing the huts with some domestic animals.

That night we made arrangements to visit a small, private astronomical observatory run by a French astronomer. He had come to visit this area several years ago, had fallen in love with it and had decided that he could use his professional background to make a good living. He bought a piece of land some distance from town so that the place was not affected by its lights. He built a house on the land and installed some telescopes. We met in his office in the town and were taken to his house by a small bus. There were about ten tourists in the group. When we arrived, he served us hot chocolate, and gave us a general lecture on astronomy. He explained why we shall never have contacts with beings in other galaxies, because they are so far away. Finally, we went outside to observe the moon and other planets through the telescopes. The astronomer was an engaging speaker who made the whole thing very entertaining and informational. We enjoyed the night and the celestial bodies that we saw through the telescopes.

The next morning we drove to Calama to catch our flight to Santiago. We wished that we could have stayed a few more days. By this time we had learned that there were several other tours available, some going into Bolivia. Despite our longing to see more, we were grateful that we had seen this most extraordinary part of the world.

PART III

COSTA RICA AND GUATEMALA

CHAPTER 11

COSTA RICA: BRIDGE BETWEEN
NORTH AND SOUTH AMERICA

Somehow I always associate Costa Rica with Gerson da Silva, a tax expert from Minas Gerais, Brazil. I described him in one of the chapters on Brazil. Da Silva had been my boss when I was a consultant for the Joint Tax Program of the IDB, OAS, and UN. He was the very articulate and imaginative man who had graduated in medicine but had convinced himself that he could help the world more working as a tax expert than as a medical doctor. I recall that he used to refer to Costa Rica as a pilot project for other countries. Especially four decades, ago Costa Rica clearly deserved that designation. This small country had decided not to have an army and had established a well-functioning democracy in a part of the world where democracies were rare. Costa Rica always spent an unusually large share of its public budget on education and health, producing socio-economic indicators far superior to those of other Central American countries and comparable to those of much richer countries. In 2005, the last year for which the indicators are available, it ranked 48th among 177 countries, just below Croatia and Uruguay. Its life expectancy and adult literacy rate were remarkably high. Education is a major national preoccupation in this country. Everyone, rich and poor, wants to have educated children.

I visited Costa Rica three times, the first to attend a conference. The second time was to head a technical assistance mission from the IMF to write a report on reforming the Costa Rican tax system. The third was to participate in a seminar with the Costa Rican "Asamblea Legislativa," that is the Costa Rican one-chamber Parliament.

At the conference on economic policy, which took place at a time when reliance on the market was increasing in popularity, Anne Krueger gave a forceful talk about the benefits of free trade for a country. At that time, Krueger was a professor of economics at Stanford University and she later became First Deputy Managing Director of the IMF. She argued that in every country there are many unknown *potential* exporters who could become *actual* exporters if a more competitive open trade policy were introduced. Such a policy would give easier access to imported inputs, necessary to produce exports, by removing quotas and other quantitative restrictions and by reducing import duties. A free trade policy would make the exchange rate more advantageous to exporters. She mentioned Turkey as a country that at that time had seen its exports grow rapidly after it had opened its frontiers to trade.

Krueger introduced some arguments from the theory of public choice that were first made by Machiavelli five hundred years ago and were popularized by Milton Friedman fifty years ago. She argued that the main obstacle to the introduction of good policies is that the losers from these policies can be easily identified, and they know that they are going to lose from the policy changes, while the winners are more difficult to identify, are a broader group, and often do not even know that they will be winners. Thus, they cannot organize in support of these policies. In the case of trade liberalization, the potential exporters are unknown and, thus, cannot create a pressure group in favor of opening the country to trade. They are often not aware of the potential role that they might play in a different trade environment. On the other hand, those who benefit from a highly regulated trade regime, as for example the producers of import substitutes, are a clearly identified, powerful lobby that can easily organize itself and prevent the introduction of policies aimed at freeing trade.

Several influential economists attended the conference, such as Francisco Gil-Diaz who later became Minister of Finance of Mexico, Stanley Fischer who would become First Deputy Managing Director of the IMF and later governor of the Central Bank of Israel, and John Williamson, who would give the name of Washington Consensus to the movement to reintroduce market principles in policymaking. In the twenty years since the conference, two trends have taken place in the world. First, the arguments for freer trade or, better, for regional integration, which may not necessarily be the same thing, have become somewhat more popular, especially in Latin America, This has led to a lowering of trade restrictions and to various agreements on trade liberalization among groups of countries. This development has in turn created some concern about the impact of trade liberalization, which requires the lowering of trade taxes, on public revenue. Second, as a counter to this development, some strong voices have been raised against globalization in its various forms, such as freer trade. Some economists, including Joe Stiglitz, Paul Krugman, and Dani Rodrik, have argued that trade liberalization may not always be as positive a development as its advocates claim. Other writers, such as Professor Amy Chua from Yale University, have argued that globalization, in its various expressions, tends to benefit those who are more prepared to take advantage of it. If these groups are ethnically different from the main population (Chinese in the Philippines and Indonesia, Lebanese or Indians in some African countries), improvement in their absolute and relative position vis-à-vis the general population will bring resentment, even when the policy change increases the countries' growth rates. Poverty cannot be seen only as an absolute concept but also as a relative one. It is thus not surprising that globalization has raised questions, at least in some people's minds, about the merit of the so-called Washington Consensus. Now in the middle of the 2008-2009 economic crisis, this Consensus is being seriously tested. The impact of the crisis on free trade and other aspects of globalization remains to be seen.

My second trip to Costa Rica took place in April 1990. It was a technical assistance mission on the part of the International Monetary Fund to advise the Costa Rican authorities on a possible reform of its tax system. The objectives of these missions were often to make the tax system of a country (a) more productive in terms of revenue; (b) more efficient in the sense of being less of an obstacle to the economic growth; (c) more equitable, if it was believed that the tax burden was not fairly distributed among different groups; and (d) more easily administrable, if the burden on the tax authorities and the cost of compliance on the taxpayers were considered high. It was generally the minister of finance of the country that set the main objectives for the mission's work.

Like most Fund missions of this type, its composition was multinational. In addition to myself, it included: Partho Shome, whom I previously mentioned, Adolfo Atchabahian, an Argentine tax expert who had been a director of the IDB-OAS-UN Joint Tax Program; and Manuel Beytia, a Chilean who had been Chile's director of taxation. After a couple of weeks of hard work, the mission produced a book-length report. The report called attention to the surprising complexity of the Costa Rican tax system and to the extremely high number of taxes (almost three hundred) used by the system.

This high number of taxes was due to the so-called process of earmarking (i.e. assigning) the specific revenue from each tax to a particular purpose. This at times created unusual outcomes. For example, a tax earmarked for the Supreme Court of Costa Rica had produced so much revenue that the Court had built a large headquarters in which each judge had a full floor. We also called attention to the widespread use of tax incentives that made it difficult to understand the impact of the system on the economy and on different income groups, reducing the transparency of the system. The report called for a process of reform aimed at reducing the number of taxes, eliminating most of the earmarking and the incentives, and increasing the simplicity and the transparency of the system. This would require the elimination of many taxes and many tax incentives. At the same time the scope of the public sector activities would also need to be reduced.

The report made many technical recommendations that cannot be summarized here for reasons of complexity and confidentiality, although it is difficult to claim that a two decades old report of this type would still contain confidential information. These technical assistance reports were considered confidential reports of the Fund to the countries' authorities. Only specific individuals within the IMF and the country's authorities could make them public. This is a pity because their greater circulation would widen their impact by educating a wider public. It also removes from public view an important activity of the IMF. On the other hand, their confidentiality makes the authorities more willing to provide information that might be considered embarrassing. In my last trip to Costa Rica in August 2003, I was happy to find out that some of the report's recommendations had been implemented (i.e. the elimination of many unproductive taxes) while others had been incorporated in recent national reform proposals. Furthermore, the report continued to have an educational value and was often cited within the country. Clearly the Costa Rican authorities did not consider it confidential anymore.

The writing of these technical assistance reports leave little time to the members of these missions for sightseeing or for other activities. However, I do recall a visit to one of the volcanoes and to a coffee plantation. There was also a visit to an art gallery where I tried to buy a naïf painting but we could not agree on a mutually acceptable price. Finally, there is another little episode worth reporting.

The last day of the mission we met the Minister of Finance to discuss the mission's recommendations. This was the meeting in which the head of the mission, in this case it was me, summarized its main conclusions for the minister and other authorities. We were sitting around a table in a large room in the ministry, and I was facing the Minister. Behind him there was a painting hanging from the wall. Suddenly, I had the impression that the painting was swinging on the wall. For a moment I thought that I was suffering the effects of a glass of wine I had had at lunch. But soon I concluded that the movement of the painting was real and realized that it was being caused by an earthquake. By coincidence, the day before employees at the Ministry had staged a demonstration concerning the building's safety. There were still posters left by the demonstrators complaining about the insufficient number of escape passages and that the Ministry was in an old building that was not likely to survive a strong earthquake. Obviously, we suspended the meeting and rushed to the street as quickly as we could. I cannot recall whether or not we met with the Minister again.

My third visit to Costa Rica was in August 2003. It was sponsored by the Inter-American Development Bank and involved a meeting with members of the "Asamblea Legislativa," the Costa Rican parliament made up of a single chamber. The group that came from outside Costa Rica included some senior staff of the IDB and outside experts from Argentina, such as Juan Carlos Gomez-Sabaini and Humberto Petrei, and Manuel Marfán from Chile. Sabaini and Petrei had been Vice-Ministers in Argentina and Marfán had been Minister of Finance in

Chile. At this time I had just returned from Italy where I had spent two years as an undersecretary in the Berlusconi government and was working as a consultant in the IDB.

The attendance of the *diputatos*, assemblymen or perhaps better, assembly persons because there were several women, was very good, and the discussion of high quality. Some of the discussion concerned the desirable level of the tax burden of Costa Rica which, it was argued, should be raised by at least two percent of the country's GDP, given its spending needs and its fiscal deficit. We also discussed income tax reform, in particular the possibility of changing this tax so that it applied to a global concept of income. The tax was applied to each type of income (each schedule) separately and did not tax income earned abroad. It thus applied a territorial concept of income. There was discussion of whether Costa Rica should tax all the combined income (the "global" income) with a single set of tax rates, or whether mobile, financial income should be taxed separately as it is now done in countries that have a *dual income tax*, such as Sweden and Denmark.

There was also much discussion about broadening the base of the VAT and about whether the broader base should be taxed with a single rate, as in Chile and Ecuador, or with more than one rate, as in several countries. Single rates are much more productive in terms of revenue and are much simpler to administer. However, multiple rates are more attractive to politicians who can argue that they are taking equity considerations into account in determining what to tax with higher rates. Marfán and I strongly argued for the single rate; Sabaini for more than one rate. The assembly persons did not express views, but my impression was that they would choose the less satisfactory, though politically more attractive, alternative of the multiple rates. Politicians often go for this option. Marfán and I were a bit annoyed with Sabaini for having supported this technically less satisfactory alternative but he may have known that a decision had already been made so that it was useless to argue against it.

At the end of the seminar I happened to talk to one of the *diputatos* who had followed the seminar attentively. He had a very dignified and serious look. He asked me when I was going back to Washington, and I told him that my wife would be coming from Washington later in the evening and that we intended to spend a couple of days sightseeing in

Costa Rica. He immediately volunteered to take us around. I told him that, perhaps, it would be preferable for us to take official tours and be real tourists so as not to interfere with his activities. He insisted on taking us out the next day with his wife. I had no choice but to accept, thanking him for his kindness.

The following morning he came to the hotel with his wife, a pretty and amicable lady, around 9:30 a.m. driving a minivan. He proposed to go first to a recently established biodiversity center where we would have a good first impression of Costa Rica's dense biodiversity. At the center we learned from its director that with a very small fraction of the earth's land, Costa Rica has about five percent of the earth's species. The reason is that Costa Rica's location makes it a kind of natural bridge between North and South America. Thus, it contains some species from both North and South America. The visits to this center, where we saw many butterflies, iguanas, turtles, and other species, reminded me of what I had read about Costa Rica in the novel, *Jurassic Park*. I began to imagine dinosaurs running wild in rain forests! Unfortunately, there were no rain forests on the *diputato*'s schedule.

At the end of our visit to the center, he informed us that we had been invited to a luncheon at the house of a prominent member of the Asamblea, whom I had met the day before and who had held several important public positions in the Costa Rican government. I was not happy with this development because I had made it plain to the *diputato* that I wanted to use the two free days to see Costa Rica and not to be sitting for hours at a luncheon table. After all, my wife had come all the way from Washington to see something of Costa Rica in the two free days. However, the polite part of me prevailed, especially after he assured us that the place for the luncheon was near and it would not take much time.

We spent quite some time searching for the house where the hosts had apparently just moved a couple of months earlier. We came to an area where there were mostly embassies. It did not seem to have normal, private houses. To orient ourselves, we stopped in front of a building that starkly contrasted the buildings around it. It was a building with a strong "announcement effect," to use an expression that economists occasionally use. It had enormous iron gates which must have been at least twenty feet tall. Behind the gates there was a winding staircase that led to the main building and to two smaller side small buildings. All three buildings were in white stone and, being much higher than the street, seemed to dominate the surrounding buildings. The whole thing looked very much like a mausoleum or like those monumental tombs that I had seen in the cemeteries of Genova or in Zagreb. The two black Mercedes parked in front signaled that this was clearly *not* a mausoleum.

This monument in front of us was not a mausoleum but the "house" we had been looking for. A guard opened the gate, and we climbed the stairs. Passing in front of a swimming pool that was located between the main building and the building on its left, we were taken to a smaller building on the side of the main one. This was the entertainment section of the house. It consisted of a sizeable room with a large bar and two restrooms, one for gents and one for ladies. This area was separate from the main residence so that one had to step outside and around the pool to go from it to the main residence. In case of inclement weather, this would not be practical but it allowed the possibility of having entertainment without disturbing the main section of the house.

The main residence was exquisitely decorated and furnished. Leading to the pool were French doors decorated from top to bottom with floral-designed stained glasses. Inside, one had a feeling of being a century or two behind due to the look of the "antiqued" but new furniture. All the items seemed to be manufactured with today's lightweight materials, including balsam tree, yet made to look like old European objects.

The lunch was a long affair that lasted some four hours. The host was a very charming, even though somewhat old-fashioned person. He reminded one of aristocrats of the past. Several prominent Costa Ricans had been invited to the luncheon, mostly ex-ministers and *diputatos*. A female member of the Asamblea and wife of another prominent Costa Rican who had died a few years earlier, did a lot of talking and some drinking. She made a long speech, intended to be a toast, but I could not follow her. When she finished, our escort insisted that I speak after her. I was somewhat embarrassed and in my improvised remarks I mentioned that over the years I had had some occasional links with Central America. While I was a student at Harvard, my supervisor during a summer job in Washington, had been Alvaro Magaña, who later became President of El Salvador. I had also worked with various tax experts from Central America, such as Arturo Corleto, Raul Goches, and Oscar Bueso, at the Joint Tax Program of the OAS-IDB-UN. I remembered all of them as pleasant individuals. I also remembered the drinking habit of some of them although I did not mention this characteristic in my speech. I ended up with a toast from Kazakhstan that I once heard at a seminar at Georgetown University and that I had come to like a lot: "the past is history, the future is a mystery, the present is a gift." So "carpe diem" as the Romans used to say; seize the day.

Around 5:00 PM we finally took leave. By this time I was annoyed that we had spent so much time eating, drinking, and talking instead of sightseeing. I mentioned to our *cicerone* that my wife was tired and would like to return to the hotel. The *diputato*, who had had many drinks by this time, ignored my request and insisted that we visit some of his friends in a nearby town. This was the last thing that we would have liked to do but our insistence in returning to the hotel fell on deaf ears. After leaving the house our escort took us on a frightening ride on the main highway through the peak load traffic. At times he drove his large van like a maniac. While we were on the road, the *diputato* received a call on his cell-phone and addressed the caller repeatedly as "presidente." He told the caller that he had with him the Italian Minister of Finance. He passed the phone to me and I had to talk to the "presidente" without knowing who he was or what he was "presidente" of. I tried to be polite, and the gentleman on the phone was very courteous and formal. He thanked me for helping Costa Rica. It turned out that the caller was an ex-president of Costa Rica.

At one point during the trip the *diputato* drove in the wrong direction of a very busy road. We almost collided head-on with a large bus. But this near collision did not make him slow down. He continued in the wrong direction on to the exit ramp until we reached the main road, fortunately still in one piece. At that point our guide casually remarked that he had not wanted to go the additional 1500 feet to take the legitimate exit. That is why he had taken the one way street in the wrong direction.

With luck and after a long ride we arrived at his "friends'" house. The friends, a couple, were waiting outside the house ready to go somewhere. That somewhere turned out to be the Lyons Club of the particular town where they lived. We found out that our guide represented that town in the Assembly. The friends got in their car, and we went to the Club in separate vehicles. Soon the town's mayor and several other individuals joined us. The *diputado* kept introducing me as the Italian Minister of Finance, in spite of my attempts to set the record straight that I had been an undersecretary and had resigned from the post. The drinking continued with many hard drinks. Our guide kept drinking one whiskey after another, and I kept thinking that he was going to drive the van to bring us back to the hotel. Would we make it back to the hotel alive?

In addition, the *diputato* had already planned to take us around the following day. He said that it would include a political activity. I kept telling him that we would prefer to take an official tour so that we could see something of Costa Rica. But he, who by now had completely changed from the dignified, serious gentleman I had met the day before into a backslapping and rough guy, was just paying no attention to what I was saying and kept drinking.

Around 8:30 p.m., I told his wife with more insistence that my wife was really very tired and that we needed to go. She volunteered to drive us together with the wife of the "friends" we had met. In spite of some complaints from the *diputato* and the others, we took leave and finally returned to the hotel. My wife and I were happy to be back safely and discussed what to do about the next day. The *diputato* had said he would call around 9:00 am to arrange the program for the day. However, we made up our minds that definitely, regardless of hard feelings, we would go on our own. We tried to get an early tour at the hotel but the only tour we could get in was at 11:00. We signed up for it anyway. To our great relief, by 11:00 a.m. the *diputato* had not yet called; he must not have been sober enough to get up early that morning. So, we happily went on our tour of the rainforest. I was relieved that I did not need to be unpleasant to the host.

The visit to the rain forest turned out to be fascinating, pleasant and highly educational. We had never been in a rain forest. As I reported in the chapters on Brazil, a few years earlier, I had spent only a few minutes at the entrance of the rain forest along the Amazon before giving up because of the wrong shoes I was wearing. The guide was a young man who spoke English well so that my wife could follow him. He told us a lot about the ecology of rainforests. We learned about *foresta nuvosa* and *foresta pluviosa* and about their role in the ecological balance of the world. We took a truly spectacular and enjoyable ride on a funicular that takes you over the forest at two different levels for a few miles. At the lower level you are right in the middle of the forest so that many trees tower over you. At the higher level you are just above the forest so that the vegetation is all below you. The open gondola moves slowly so that one can observe the splendor of the vegetation under and around, listen to the guides' explanation, and take pictures. You can also distinctly hear the extraordinary symphony made by the inhabitants of the forest. The trip lasts a couple of hours. It was raining, as one would expect in a rain forest, and at the entrance we had bought plastic ponchos to protect ourselves from the light rain. After the gondola ride we walked for another hour along a narrow paved path through the forest and even saw a poisonous snake. We enjoyed the walk but the gondola ride was far more interesting.

On the way back to San Jose, it had stopped raining, and the sky had cleared. We had a spectacular view of the Poa volcano and learned that Costa Rica, in its small area, has one hundred twelve volcanoes, five of which are active. In 1963, on the day when President Kennedy arrived in Costa Rica for a state visit, one of these volcanoes erupted and the eruption continued for two years. This eruption threw millions of tons of volcanic dust in the air, covering roads, houses, and fields and transforming days into nights. The lands that were covered with the volcanic dust lost their crop that year. However, in successive years they acquired phenomenal productivity.

We returned to Washington regretting that we did not have an opportunity to see some of the volcanoes and more of this extraordinary country. A few days after our return we heard that one of the volcanoes had erupted.

CHAPTER 12

GUATEMALA: KIDNAPPERS AND THE POPE'S VISIT

To commemorate the Golden Jubilee (50ᵗʰ Anniversary) of the Central Bank of Guatemala, the Bank invited me to deliver a lecture on Fiscal Policy and Growth. The conference would take place in June of 1996. I decided to take my son, Giancarlo, with me and to spend three days sightseeing. The people at the Central Bank were kind enough to make arrangements for the trip. The morning of our departure from Washington, we ran into a small crisis. Giancarlo discovered that his U.S. passport would be expiring soon. At the travel office of the IMF they told me that he might get in trouble because the airlines wanted passports that do not expire for six months. We went to the U.S. Passport Office to try to get the passport renewed in a couple of hours and found out that just going through the line would take that long. Budgetary stringency often has an effect on private costs. At times, when a government tries to save money, it just shifts the burden on the citizens. It had not been that way for passports in the past. The waiting time to get a passport had become much longer. I recalled that some years earlier I had applied for a new passport and had received it the next day in the mail! Fortunately, because of his mother's nationality, Giancarlo also had a French passport that he could use.

We took a chance and went to the airport. The people at American Airlines had no problems with the US passport, and we got on the plane. We had seats in first class, but they only served a turkey sandwich

184

showing that the definition of first class is a relative one. Well, times change and not just in the government! We had to change planes in Miami. There we ran into Rudi Dornbusch, then a well known economist and Professor at MIT, who was going to the same conference. As usual he was very nice. We discussed the decline in the quality of food served in planes, and he said that he routinely asked in advance for a plate of fruits. He remembered my key and locks collection and told me that he had seen some interesting locks in Ecuador but that he did not know enough to determine just how good they were. I invited him to come to see my collection the next time he was in Washington. Some months later Dornbusch mailed me a lock that he had bought in Ecuador. Unfortunately, the envelope arrived without the lock. The envelope had been opened and the lock removed. There must have been another lock collector in the Post Office! Sadly Rudi died a few years later at the peak of his career.

Dornbusch was the first speaker at the Guatemala Central Bank's Golden Jubilee. He spoke on Inflation and Growth, a topic of still great relevance at the time. How important is it to push the inflation rate down to low levels in developing countries? His view was that it was not worth pushing the inflation rate below fifteen percent per year because the cost of this reduction is just too high. There was at the time some empirical evidence showing that inflation below forty percent per year did not have much of an effect on growth. Many people challenged this conclusion. I personally had major doubts that an inflation rate at that level would not affect growth through the many distortions that it would generate in areas such as the financial market, the tax system, and prices.

The flight to Guatemala had been uneventful. We were met at the airport and taken by car to Antigua, about an hour away. All the way to Antigua it was raining hard and the visibility was very poor. We got to Antigua and were taken to the Hotel Casa Santo Domingo, which had opened five years earlier in a restored sixteenth century monastery. It is truly one of the most fabulous hotels I have ever seen. It managed to keep the feel of a monastery to the extent that in the evening there were no electrical lights in the common areas including the restaurant but only candles. Giancarlo and I had a nice dinner by candlelight with piped music of monastic chants. Furthermore, and this was more good news, it was not very expensive.

The hotel covers a large area that includes some interesting ruins. There are fountains and works of art mainly with a pre-colonial Mayan character. Most likely the monastery was built on top of some pre-Columbian temple. Even the music was fit for a monastery. I had seen similar hotels—the Libertador in Cuzco, the Camino Real in Puebla, Mexico, and the Hotel San Domenico Palace in Taormina, Italy—but the Casa Santo Domingo was the most genuine and charming of the hotels built on restored old monasteries. It was definitely the hotel to stay in Antigua.

Antigua itself, the oldest Central American metropolis, is an incredible, historical town. Tragically, a large part of it was destroyed in 1976 by a horrible earthquake that killed thousands of people. Only the façades of many beautiful churches were left standing. Still the city retains a great charm and character. The Plaza de Armas is the typical Spanish colonial square with the municipal building, the Cathedral, and the police station. These were the symbols of power in Spanish colonial times and they are found in many Latin American old towns.

The following morning we drove and walked through much of the city. A visit to the ruins of San Francisco monastery, which cover a huge area, was extremely worthwhile. This must have been an extraordinary complex, almost a little town. Traces of paintings and beautiful carvings are still visible everywhere. The monasteries must have played a very important role in the economy of some earlier societies, with a large proportion of the population living or working in them. I have not seen a good study on the economic role of monasteries in the past. It would make a good topic for a research. I took many pictures that, I hoped, would do justice to the complex. We went back to the hotel for a pleasant lunch in one of its gardens and admired the many parrots and fountains that adorned the gardens.

In the afternoon, we left for Atitlan. The road to Atitlan was crowded with cars and trucks continually playing Russian roulette with incoming traffic on the dangerous mountain road. The results of this game were visible on the side of the road as we frequently saw crosses placed where someone had been killed in a crash or where a car had gone off the cliff. Multiple crosses meant multiple deaths, often off of a cliff. We saw a near miss between a bus and an incoming truck and saw a car that had to move to the left shoulder of the road when its attempt to pass another car at a curve was cut short by incoming traffic. Drivers seemed to be largely indifferent to the risk of being killed. I could not help wondering whether attitude toward risk, including that related to driving, is related to the level of per capita income. Do people become more careful as the quality of their life improves? I do not know whether economics or sociology has provided an answer to this question. People seem to be more prudent in wealthier societies but this may be the result of better enforced rules. But then why do richer countries choose stricter rules?

We arrived in Atitlan in the midst of rain and a lot of fog. The poor visibility made it difficult to enjoy the sights. We hoped that the following day would be nicer for our visit to the famous market of Chichicastenango (Chichi) and to see the beauty of Lake Atitlan. We went to the Hotel Atitlan and got a room that had a view of the lake and the volcanoes, but the weather prevented us from seeing much. A group of Italians had also arrived to the hotel, and, as expected from Italians, they were making a lot of noise. The next morning we left for Chichi but before leaving we had another look at the lake and the volcanoes. In spite of the limited visibility the view was breathtaking.

The way to Chichicastanango is very mountainous with lots of curves and steep slopes. It is not a road for the faint of heart. In many places you can see the recent effects of landslides on the road. Near Chichi the road became very congested. I saw buses squeezing near other buses and often missing them by inches. The drivers must develop very good hand-eye coordination in this part of the world. When we reached Chichi, we parked the car at a corner. The driver had to stay with the car because our luggage was clearly visible in the station wagon and we did not want to leave it unattended even in a locked car.

We walked, trying to keep our sense of direction. The market was a labyrinth full of traditional things such as food, live animals, clothes, spices, and utensils. It was a very colorful market that gave us a feel for the country. This is a place where the still prevalent Maya culture meets the modern world but it seems that the modern world is still no match for that culture. One senses that the modern world has only coated the traditional world. As I had felt in other Latin American areas, the deeper you go, the more you find the old culture.

We visited a famous Christian church in Chichi, where strange rites, which seemed to have little to do with Christianity, were taking place. Here the indigenous Maya population has mixed Christian rites with pre-Columbian ones and, probably, Christian gods with Maya gods. When we came out of the church, it was raining. It soon intensified and became a downpour. We waited a while, but it was obvious that the rain was not going to stop. We decided to dash for the car, stopping on the way under any tent that provided some protection from the rain. We lost our sense of direction so that it took some time to find the car. By that time we were completely drenched. A torrential rain was coming down as hard as I had rarely seen rain before. We decided to leave for Guatemala City.

The road back must have given us one of the most dangerous rides of our lives. The mountain roads were tortuous and steep, and many cars were driving dangerously on the road. The rain had formed torrents that crossed the road in many areas and threatened to take some cars with them down the mountain. The ever-present risk of landslides had been increased by the rain. Fortunately, our driver was a careful one. It took four hours to get to Guatemala City, and the weather hardly changed, though the road improved once we left the mountains. On the road, there were often people, mostly women and children, drenched by the rain walking towards unknown destinations. I felt sorry for them and lucky to have the protection of a car. I could not help thinking how different my life was from theirs. When we got to Guatemala City, we were taken to the Camino Real, a nice but rather uninteresting hotel in the middle of the city. My son, Giancarlo, having sat for many hours in the car, was bored by now and became a bit restless. We had a light dinner at the hotel café and went to sleep.

The next morning I went to the Central Bank, where I was to give my lecture. When I arrived, Vittorio Corbo, a Chilean economist who had been at the World Bank and was to become President of the Central Bank of Chile, was speaking on the impact of globalization on macroeconomic policy. I was impressed by his power-point presentation, a technique that was still new at that time. Within a few years power-point presentations would become *de rigueur* and one would feel very dated giving a simple talk in the way people had done for thousands of years. I still distinctly recall the first time I used the technique after this conference. I even kept track of the date. It clearly makes it much easier for the speaker and probably also helps the audience to absorb the information aurally and visually. However, I still have mixed feelings about whether it improves or reduces the transfer of information. It spares one the need to write a well-articulated paper for conferences. It also makes it more difficult to publish edited books from conferences because some people never translate the power point presentation in full articulated papers. At times the power-points have been prepared by assistants of the speakers. I would guess that in recent years the percentage of edited books from conferences has declined. At times the aesthetic quality of the power-point presentation hides the limited quality of the ideas. The power-point can provide a kind of beautiful package for poor or limited content.

Vittorio Corbo was followed by the President of the Central Bank of Guatemala, Willy Zapota, who talked about fiscal policy in Guatemala. He argued that at eight percent of GDP, the tax level of Guatemala at the time was much too low to generate the revenue necessary to improve the lot of the indigenous population. This commitment to improve conditions for indigenous people had been agreed upon in the Pacto Social, that would be officially signed on December 29, 1996, with the Unidad Revolucionaria Nacional Guatemalteca (URNG), which had ended 36 years of internal fighting. A large share of the indigenous population did not go to school and did not have the most basic services because these were not available where they lived. It was questionable whether their income was higher than at the time of the Mayas. The Pacto Social, *inter alia*, related to the level of public revenue, to the quality of the tax system, to the need for more transparency in the use of resources, and for more efficiency in public spending. The need for these reforms was underscored by the fact that in the conference room there were some five hundred persons, but not a single one seemed to be of Indian (Maya) descent. These people seemed not to exist in spite of the fact that they represented about half of the population of Guatemala.

My lecture followed that of the President of the Central Bank. I had been asked to talk on "fiscal policy and growth." I tried to outline the various channels through which fiscal policy can affect growth—through level and structure of taxation, and level and structure of spending or through the existence of fiscal deficits. I mentioned that Guatemala's current tax level was among the lowest in the world. The country would gain in efficiency and growth by taxing more and spending more in badly-needed, productive, and socially relevant activities. I reminded the audience of a slogan I had seen on the road from Chichicastenango: "niña educada: madre del desarrollo," or "an educated child is the mother of development." There is in fact a lot of literature that has established a direct link between the education of women who will become mothers and thus their children's first teachers, and economic development. Children are not born educated; the government has a responsibility in making them so. I argued that there was a basic need for more public spending on primary education and basic health and other essential government services. The extremely uneven distribution of income in Guatemala made this public spending and higher level of taxation absolute necessities.

My intervention was followed by that of the Minister of Finance who mentioned only the need to improve tax administration to reduce tax evasion. For him the tax system and the level of the tax rates were okay, only tax administration needed to be improved. Over the next four years, the ratio of tax revenue to gross domestic product (T/TGDP) would need to increase by four percent of GDP to allow the increase in social expenditure for health and primary education agreed in the peace treaty with the guerrillas. The armed conflict had lasted from 1960 to 1996 and had caused the death or disappearance of some two hundred thousand people. Improvements in tax administration were not likely to generate significant tax increases. By 2003, the T/TGDP had risen to about 10.5 percent, largely as a result of successful administrative improvements. This level was still much too low and was still some distance from the goal of twelve percent of GDP agreed in the Pacto Social. By the way Guatemala was ranked 118th on the UNDP's Human Development Index in 2005. In 2003, a U.N. mission had concluded that some of the commitments made in the Pacto Social remained unmet. Furthermore, after reaching 10.5 percent of GDP, the tax level had started going down again. In more recent years it did rise to twelve percent of GDP.

In the following round table with the President of the Central Bank, the Minister, Corbo, and myself, we addressed some of these same themes. I was also asked about corruption, a topic to which I was paying a lot of attention at that time and was pushing the IMF to become more concerned and vocal about it. This was also a significant problem in Guatemala.

At the luncheon given by the President of the Central Bank, I learned several interesting facts about Guatemala from the people at my table. I learned:

(a) About the deep division within the government on economic policies. This had been obvious in the interventions of the President of the Central Bank and the Minister of finance;

(b) About the oligarchy unwilling to increase taxes. This oligarchy was made up of a group of relatively few families that controlled much of Guatemala's resources. Its members had a lot of influence on who went into the government and, thus, had a lot of control over government policies;

(c) That the Supreme Court had found an increase in electricity prices to be against "civil rights;"

(d) About the kidnapping industry that had developed with several kidnappings per day. This seemed to be the main growth industry in Guatemala at that time. Some individuals were contacted by kidnapping gangs and asked to pay a kidnapping charge: a kind of insurance premium against being kidnapped! This technique was similar to that of the Mafia that asked for a charge against the risk of having a shop burned. The premium included a discount because the kidnapping had not yet occurred so there had been no costs for the kidnappers. Thus, the "savings" could be passed on to the prospective kidnapping victim. Economists would say that in this case this payment created mainly a problem of distribution and not of allocation as long as no actual kidnapping took place and as long as people did not respond by buying protection, that is hiring bodyguards;

(e) That in one case, a young man had been kidnapped and his mother had been contacted and asked for a specific ransom. She had replied that she was willing to pay all the money that she had, but this was less than the amount asked. The reply came that her proposal could not be accepted because the head of the gang of kidnappers had gone to see the Pope who was visiting Guatemala on that day and only the head could negotiate a reduction in the price of ransom. When the head came back, he refused the counter-offer, explaining to the lady that he was planning to retire soon from his activity and had a target value for the assets he needed for his retirement. He needed the full ransom to achieve his goal. I could not find out what happened to the kidnapped victim!

(f) That the kidnappers used the "ability to pay principle" to determine a fair ransom. The ransom was set according to the estimated wealth of the family of the kidnapped. They seemed to have better information than the tax authorities on the families' wealth and income. By the way this is an argument for keeping income tax declarations confidential and for maintaining bank secrecy. The Swiss have used it occasionally;

(g) That experienced criminals were moving to Costa Rica from Guatemala bringing with them their acquired skills. This was a good example of the globalization of crime or of the cross-country transfer of know-how.

Kidnapping has been a major problem in many Latin American countries and especially in Colombia, where the Department of National Planning has reported that in the period between 1996 and 2003 twenty-one thousand persons had been kidnapped. In recent years it became a serious problem in Argentina. In fact, lack of security is often mentioned as the number one problem in Latin America in yearly surveys reported in Latino-barometers.

At 6:00 a.m. the next day, we left for the airport to catch our flight to Tikal, the famous Mayan ruin. The plane was just a box with propellers and it left fifteen minutes ahead of schedule. The flight to Tikal (by Tikal Jets!) was smooth. Our guide, Carlos, met us and assembled a group for a minibus. The ride to the ruins took about one hour. It was hot and humid, but not unbearably so. We arrived at Tikal and began the trek through the rain forest. Some of the trees were huge and hundreds of years old. The variety of vegetation and of birds was extraordinary. There are apparently two hundred and fifty kinds of birds in Guatemala and many of them seemed to be in the trees around us. They made the most beautiful symphony.

On the tour, I struck up a conversation with an American, who turned out to be a professor of economics at a small college in South Carolina. He said that he was in Guatemala to teach public choice at the national university. Public choice is a field of economics (or some would say of political science) originally developed by James Buchanan, the Nobel prize winning conservative American economist. Public choice is also linked to the writings of various Italian economists—such as Mazzola, Pantaleone, Fasiani, Nitti, Pareto, Puviani and others—in the early part of the twentieth century. These writers had not accepted the premise, common to Anglo-Saxon or North European writers, that the role of the government is basically a benevolent one aimed at improving the welfare, or the well being, of the citizens.

Buchanan had spent a sabbatical year in Italy in 1957 and had been influenced by the writing of these economists and by the Italian "Scienza delle Finanze." In some ways, it could be argued that he owed his Nobel Prize to that sabbatical year. Public choice tries to apply economic tools to explain why governments often fail in their attempt to solve problems or to correct for failures of the market. Public choice economists believe that clientelism, self interest, rent seeking, and corruption often influence public policy and cause it to generate poor results. They conclude that when the government intervenes to correct the market, it replaces market failure with government failure, and government failure may be worse than market failure. Thus, they are against government and especially against large and central governments. Buchanan has been a strong advocate of fiscally decentralized governments.

The professor complained that the students did not seem to be impressed with, or interested in, the American examples. I pointed out to him that, with taxation at only eight percent of GDP, Guatemala was unlikely to need less government but rather more and better government. I did not change his views. He insisted that Guatemala had too much government.

Our conversation came to a sudden end as we entered the Main Plaza. It is one of the most extraordinary sights anywhere. Two huge Temples (Temple I and Temple II) face each other on the Plaza. This was the heart of the ancient city of Tikal. Temple I rises about 170 feet above the ground. It is a magnificent structure often called the Temple of the Giant Jaguar. It was built around 700 AD. The temple is in the form of a pyramid with nine sloping terraces, nine being a sacred number for the Maya. By any standards, it is an extraordinary and stunning building, itself worth the trip to Guatemala. Across from Temple I, Temple II is a smaller and less slim version of Temple I. It is 125 feet tall and easier to climb. The walls of the rooms are covered by drawings, some showing human sacrifices. The other two sides of the plaza contain monumental terraces and in front of one of them there are *steles,* that is stone slabs that were elaborately carved.

I tried to imagine what had taken place in that plaza over many years. Human sacrifices? Games? Religious ceremonies? Sacrifices of slaves or enemies, or of beautiful girls? If the most beautiful girls were chosen for sacrifices by the Maya, the Incas, and the Aztecs, as it is sometimes claimed, what impact did this have, over the long run, on the appearance of these races? I wondered! Recent archeological discoveries have confirmed the great role that blood spilling had in Maya culture. Not only enemies captured but even the local aristocrats engaged routinely in blood-spilling ceremonies. The blood was offered to the gods, who must have been considered blood thirsty.

From the great plaza we walked to Temple IV which is the greatest of the Tikal religious buildings. It stands at 212 feet, higher than any other pre-Columbian building. It must have been the Empire State Building of pre-Columbus America. It is difficult to access; one has to climb an almost vertical wall covered with the roots of trees that provide a grip to lift oneself. My son, Giancarlo, went up and he was extremely happy that he did. I thought that I was too old to do it so I stayed behind. He reported that the view from the top was breathtaking. The acoustics in the area are also fantastic. I could have a conversation with my son from almost two hundred yards away. He insisted that he could even hear a big cat, perhaps a puma, growling. The building is so massive that it is estimated to have required a huge amount of construction material. This temple was also built around 741 AD.

We walked around the area for another couple of hours, visiting other less impressive but still remarkable sights. The question that inevitably comes to mind is why this fascinating city was suddenly abandoned after fifteen hundred years of history, a history that started about 600 BC? Clearly something happened around 900 AD that caused the place to be largely abandoned. Was it a plague? Overexploitation? Earthquake? Drought? Various theories have been advanced over the years. Recently some convincing evidence has been presented which points to a major drought that dried the reservoirs and made it impossible to keep producing the crops needed for the population of this and other large Mayan cities. This area has neither rivers, nor lakes, nor underground water. Thus, it depends on the yearly rain and on the accumulation of that rain in reservoirs. A drought lasting several years would make survival impossible.

The history of the Maya must be a fascinating one. Not much is known about them, especially about those who occupied Tikal. However, they had writing and left some historical records. It is known that they were advanced in mathematics and astronomy. They already knew the existence of zero. They performed difficult surgery. They were obviously great builders. It was a civilization without the wheel and without money, as other civilizations of the Americas. However, it is not likely that the wheel would have been very useful because, before the Europeans arrived with horses, there were no animals that could have pulled a cart with wheels. Money, too, probably would not have been very useful in a society with pre-assigned roles for everyone. The area of Tikal uncovered so far is perhaps only about ten percent of the ruins known to be buried under the jungle. The city was a large one by ancient standards, with perhaps eighty thousand inhabitants. It had markets, drainage systems and a large water reservoir. A map at the airport indicated at least eighty archeological sites. We saw only a few of them.

There are many good books on the Maya, such as *The Rise and Fall of Maya Civilization*, by J. Eric S. Thompson. An earlier one is *The Ancient Maya*, written by Silvanus Griswold Morley. The National Geographic Society has also dedicated many publications to these mysterious people.

In the afternoon we flew back to Guatemala City by the same plane. The flight was once again fairly smooth. When we got to Guatemala City, it was raining. I wish we had spent a night at Tikal to revisit the sights we saw and to visit some other ones. The area is so rich with ruins that one could spend weeks or even months going from one to the other. I promised to myself that during my retirement years I would sometime revisit this area at a more leisurely pace. However, I am still waiting for the free time to do it. I have become aware that there are two kinds of budgets in the life of a person that become constraining at different periods. One is the money budget. The other is the time budget. Often when one has plenty of time, he/she may have little money. When the money constraint is relaxed, the time constraints become operational.

When I returned to Washington, I convinced a colleague, Howell Zee, to coauthor with me a paper using my presentation at the Central Bank as the base. The resulting paper called "Fiscal Policy and Economic Growth" was published in the *IMF Staff Papers*, the academic journal of the IMF, and has been frequently cited.

CONCLUDING REMARKS

The previous chapters dealt with events that stretched over at least four decades. It may be worthwhile to add a few concluding thoughts and to point to very recent developments in some of the countries covered by the book before bringing it to a close.

Until last year, Brazil had been riding the favorable wave of the commodity boom that sharply increased its foreign earnings. This allowed it to pay most of its external debt and reduced the economic difficulties that it had experienced in earlier years. Inflation had been under control and the economy had been growing at low rates. Brazil had also benefited from the discovery of sizeable oil deposits on its continental shelf and from its efficient and growing production of ethanol. In a world where energy has become the lifeblood of economic activities, these latter developments are very important and will help the country in the future. At the political level its associations with a group of very large and fast growing countries, the BRIC—a group that includes also Russia, India, and China—has raised its political visibility and importance in the world. It is no longer seen as a relatively poor and badly managed developing country. The future may have finally arrived for Brazil. It now seems destined to slowly come to dominate economically, and perhaps even politically, South America, in a way that the United States has dominated the Northern part of the American continent. If this happens, Brazil would become a counter weight in the Americas to the United States.

Its current president, Luiz Inácio Lula da Silva, has proven to be far more pragmatic than many had expected, or feared, when he was elected. He has initiated some new programs aimed at improving the very unequal income distribution of Brazil that had characterized the country over the years. These programs have helped him remain popular. He has also maintained a generally orthodox macroeconomic policy

Peru has also been riding a good economic wave and in recent years has been growing at the fastest rate in Latin America. In 2009 Alberto Fujimori, the former president of Peru of Japanese background, who had dominated Peruvian developments during much of the decade of the 1990s and who escaped to Japan after being accused of corruption, was brought back to Peru and tried for corruption and other crimes. He was found guilty and sent to jail. Alan García, the leftist president who, rightly or wrongly, had been blamed for much of the economic difficulties of Peru in the second half of the 1980s, was re-elected president and, this time around, turned out to be far more pro-market than anyone had expected. He has become a darling of the IMF because of the good macroeconomic policies that Peru has been following. Unfortunately, the problems of highly uneven income distribution and the differential income levels of different ethnic groups and different regions of the country remain unsolved. Recently, García was faced with strong, armed resistance, on the part of some indigenous groups, against development plans that would open some areas of the interior of the country for commercial activities and explorations. These activities would bring more employment and more foreign currency to the country but would also bring potentially major environmental problems, as previous oil exploitations had done. The chapters on Peru had predicted that this was likely to become a growing problem for the governments of Peru and of other countries with similar heterogeneous populations.

In Chile, Michelle Bachelet came to the presidency with a more leftist reputation than her predecessor. She became president of a country with good institutions and good policies. Chile has also benefited enormously from the commodity boom that over many years kept high the price of its major export, copper. The previous Chilean government had created a "development fund" that allowed the country to save the extra foreign earnings, rather than spend it immediately. This meant that the country would be able to survive a period of economic recession without major economic and social difficulties.

In recent months there had been more talk about corruption in Chile than had normally been the case. This is a worrisome development because Chile has been considered the least corrupted country in Latin America. Hopefully this talk may not reflect a genuine worsening on this ground. With the good policies of past years, and the continually good performance of its institutions, Chile can be expected to move, at a good speed, toward a place among the countries that make up the so-called developed world. Its institutions are already at that level. Its per capita income and its income distribution still have a way to go.

In a recent survey, Costa Rica was classified as one of the happiest countries in the world. Whether or not this ranking is correct, Costa Rica remains a kind of "pilot project" for other developing countries and especially for other countries from Central America. It continues to have a high life expectancy, good educational standards, a reasonably good welfare system, and a true democratic political system. It receives a score well above that predicted by its per capita income in the Human Development Index prepared by the United Nations. Costa Rica has continued with its decades-long, but so far not successful attempt to reform its tax system to make it more progressive and more efficient.

Like Costa Rica, but starting far behind, Guatemala is continuing with its goal of trying to get higher public revenue in order to give more tools to the government to improve educational and social standards. The Inter-American Development Bank has published a book, entitled *Gravar Para Crecer*, or *Tax in Order to Grow*, that captures this goal. Guatemala continues to have one of the lowest tax levels in the world, in the same order of magnitude as it was in the United States and other developed countries a century ago. However, it is attempting to raise tax revenue through administrative reforms and not through policy changes. Powerful economic interests make it difficult for Guatemala to introduce policy changes that would help raise tax revenue significantly. It will be interesting to see how much progress this country will be able to make in its social objectives with so little public revenue. It is attempting to pursue a role of the state that had largely disappeared in the modern world. Regardless of this issue, Guatemala remains the most beautiful country in Central America and is a truly extraordinary place to visit.

Having spent much of my life traveling to the four corners of the world, I have become fully aware of how special Latin America is. Its natural beauty is probably unmatched elsewhere. One finds here some of the most extraordinary places on earth. Only in Latin America have I occasionally felt as if I were in another planet. The archeological sites take one's breath away. Some are as grandiose as those in Egypt and China. The population includes more diversity than I have seen anywhere else. In many places there has been little melting of the different ethnic groups in spite of the strong Spanish and Portuguese influence. The African blacks have had a major impact on the culture of many countries. At the same time while some areas are almost more European than Europe itself, some groups continue to live in the same way as they did when the Europeans first came.

I hope that this little book will encourage more people to visit this extraordinary and charming region.

INDEX OF IMPORTANT NAMES